The
Policy Analyst's
Handbook

The Policy Analyst's Handbook

Rational Problem Solving in a Political World

Lewis G. Irwin

M.E.Sharpe
Armonk, New York
London, England

Library of Congress Cataloging-in-Publication Data

Irwin, Lewis G.
    The policy analyst's handbook : rational problem solving in a political world /
by Lewis G. Irwin.
        p. cm.
    Includes bibliographical references and index.
    ISBN 0-7656-1292-5 (cloth: alk. paper) — ISBN 0-7656-1293-3 (pbk.: alk. paper)
    1. Policy sciences. 2. Policy sciences—Decision making. I. Title.

    H97.I78 2003
    320'.6—dc21   2003005329

Printed in the United States of America

The paper used in this publication meets the minimum requirements of
American National Standard for Information Sciences
Permanence of Paper for Printed Library Materials,
ANSI Z 39.48-1984.

∞

BM (c)   10   9   8   7   6   5   4   3   2   1
BM (p)   10   9   8   7   6   5   4   3   2   1

For Mary, Eva, and Andrew

Contents

Figures and Tables

Preface

The phrase "policy analysis" typically conjures up images of analysts with short-sleeved shirts, striped ties, and pocket protectors sitting in a government building, quietly poring over reams of statistics and seeking solutions to public policy problems. But while this particular notion may perhaps capture one aspect of reality in the world of policy analysis, a proper and modern definition of the phrase must encompass a much broader and more diverse view. First of all, whether we realize it or not, we all engage in policy analysis as part of our professional lives, to varying degrees and in varying ways. Furthermore, it is the rare analyst who enjoys the luxury of proceeding uninterrupted and unconstrained in a dispassionate, leisurely, and purely rational analysis of a policy problem from start to finish. Moreover, regardless of our respective fields of endeavor, we all operate in a political world in the sense that our problem solving happens within the context of competing agendas, resource constraints, deadlines, and other challenges for the would-be rational problem solver.

So we are all policy analysts of one kind or another. For some of us, formal policy analysis is a crucial part of our professional responsibilities, and decision briefings and structured problem solving play prominent roles in our daily activities. For others among us, policy analysis takes the form of the frequent though informal decision-making processes that we carry out in the context of our broader occupational responsibilities. The phrase "policy analysis" today encompasses the consideration of both public and private issues as well as the search for solutions to a wide range of problems. It is the rare professional who is not routinely required to make policy decisions or recommendations.

In addition, we all have a few important things in common, regardless of how it is that we arrive at the analytic task. For starters, we are all looking for efficient and accurate ways to process information, generate ideas, and choose from potential courses of action. And whether our particular decision-making task is more formally structured or less so, we all share the need to make rational and informed decisions in the face of the complex and shifting environments common to our modern world, whatever our area of interest or inquiry. Finally, we are all looking for ways to improve the means through which we deal with the mass of information available to us in our decision making, information that is too often imperfect, incomplete, or overwhelming as we deliberate in advance of the deadline.

With all of these points in mind, this book is designed to help you become an effective and efficient policy analyst. It also aims to achieve the larger goal of helping you solve problems in your professional life more effectively. Effective policy analysis comes from a more distinctive mindset than from anything else. This book will introduce to you a structured and disciplined approach to rational decision making and issue analysis that is quite useful in the context of the uncertain environments that we typically face. In particular, this book will enable you to deal with the dual challenges of uncertainty and prediction that make the analytic task difficult in the first place. But do not be surprised if you find yourself using some of these problem-solving techniques, or at least applying the underlying logic of the problem-solving processes in daily decision making in your personal lives. There is no reason why you shouldn't! In its essence, effective policy analysis involves injecting elements of rationality into an otherwise less than rational world, and this skill has broad applicability within a wide range of enterprises. Furthermore, because so much policy analysis is done primarily upon the basis of hunches, opinions, and predispositions, you should understand that there is a real opportunity here. The analyst who can inject that note of rationality into an otherwise less than rational process will eventually be proven right far more often than not. The truth is, some careers (such as policy analysts) are made out of less than that.

To accomplish these worthwhile objectives, the book begins with a description of the fundamental challenges of social science and the application of the scientific method to questions involving human behavior or human interaction. If you think about it, almost all of our professional endeavors fall into this broad category to one degree or another. Then, after offering these perspectives on the basic challenges posed to the policy analyst by the nature of his task, the book addresses the first critical step the effective policy analyst must take: precisely defining the problem at hand. The book then follows the analytic process from step to step, as the analyst generates potential solutions to the problem at hand, seeks information needed to define alternatives precisely, and evaluates the potential solutions in light of carefully selected evaluative criteria.

The book subsequently addresses in detail the application of the two predominant approaches to policy analysis, *cost-benefit analysis* (CBA) and *multi-attribute analysis* (MAA). In essence, CBA is a method of policy analysis most appropriate when costs or efficiency are the analyst's overriding concerns, whereas MAA works better when other values or considerations are paramount. This book aims to place the analytic task and these powerful techniques within the context of the "political world," describing the likely limits within which the effective policy analyst will have to ply his or her trade. Each chapter concludes with notes and a list of supplemental sources that elaborate upon the topics covered within that chapter. Thus, I have aimed to provide an accessible and informative description of the challenges and techniques of policy analysis while also providing a point of entry into the broader literature relevant to these fields of scholarly interest.

Acknowledgments

No work of this sort is a wholly individual undertaking, and this book is no exception to that rule. I am especially grateful for the assistance of Reed Day, Charles Rubin, Clifford Bob, and Chris Gibson in shaping this book. I also appreciate the support of my colleagues at Duquesne University and that of mentors and fellow officers in the U.S. Army, in particular those from the very special Department of Social Sciences at West Point. Further heartfelt thanks go to Patricia Kolb, Henrietta Toth, and Amy Albert at M.E. Sharpe for their vision and their assistance in seeing the project through to fruition. In many ways, it is all of you who have made this book possible. To all of you and to my wife Marcia, I am profoundly grateful for your friendship and support.

Note for Instructors

While this book can stand alone as the central text for a course in public policy analysis, its primary aim is to serve as an accessible companion text for courses in public policy, public administration, political science, sociology, and other social science courses. With this objective in mind, you can use the book to help your students in a number of ways: first, the book is an accessible guide to the fundamental principles of social scientific inquiry, and provides students with the basics of social science in a way that will enable them to grasp quickly the essence of the social scientist's central objectives; second, the book can serve as effective complement to the many fine public-policy textbooks on the market that cover the policy-making process and substantive areas of public policy but do not elaborate on the practical techniques of policy analysis; third, the book's step-by-step approach to rational public problem solving will help your students as they tackle their own policy analyses, regardless of the subject of those analyses; and finally, the book offers a survey of the literature in the field of policy analysis, thus enabling your students to find additional information on areas of interest. Here are some of the books that *The Policy Analyst's Handbook* complements well:

Anderson, James E. *Public Policymaking*, 3d ed. Boston: Houghton Mifflin, 1997.

Bonser, Charles F., Eugene B. McGregor Jr., and Clinton V. Oster Jr. *Policy Choices and Public Action*. Upper Saddle River, NJ: Prentice Hall, 1996.

Bonser, Charles F., Eugene B. McGregor Jr., and Clinton V. Oster Jr. *American Public Policy Problems: An Introductory Guide*, 2d ed. Upper Saddle River, NJ: Prentice Hall, 2000.

Brewster, Lawrence G., and Michael E. Brown. *The Public Agenda: Issues in American Politics*, 4th ed. New York: St. Martin's, 1998.

Clemons, Randall S., and Mark K. McBeth. *Public Policy Praxis: Theory and Pragmatism: A Case Approach.* Upper Saddle River, NJ: Prentice Hall, 2001.

Cochran, Clarke E., et al. *American Public Policy*, 6th ed. New York: St. Martin's/Worth, 1999.

Dye, Thomas R. *Understanding Public Policy*, 10th ed. Englewood Cliffs, NJ: Prentice Hall, 2002.

Fry, Brian R. *Mastering Public Administration.* Chatham, NJ: Chatham House, 1989.

Gordon, George J. *Public Administration in America*, 4th ed. New York: St. Martin's, 1992.

Guess, George M., and Paul G. Farnham. *Cases in Public Policy Analysis*, 2nd ed. Washington, DC: Georgetown University Press, 2000.

Heineman, Robert A., et al. *The World of the Policy Analyst: Rationality, Values, and Politics*, 3d ed. New York: Chatham House, 2002.

Hill, Michael. *The Policy Process in the Modern State*, 3d ed. New York: Prentice Hall, 1997.

Jreisat, Jamil E. *Comparative Public Administration and Policy.* Boulder, CO: Westview, 2002.

Lester, James P., and Joseph Stewart Jr. *Public Policy: An Evolutionary Approach.* Minneapolis: West, 1996.

Munger, Michael C. *Analyzing Policy: Choices, Conflicts, and Practices.* New York: Norton, 2000.

Peters, B. Guy. *American Public Policy*, 5th ed. Pittsburgh: University of Pittsburgh, 2000.

Rosenbloom, David H. *Public Administration: Understanding Management, Politics, and Law in the Public Sector*, 4th ed. New York: McGraw-Hill, 1998.

Stillman, Richard J. II. *Public Administration: Concepts and Cases*, 6th ed. Geneva, IL: Houghton Mifflin, 1996.

Stone, Deborah. *Policy Paradox: The Art of Political Decision Making*. New York: Norton, 1997.

Theodoulou, Stella A., and Matthew A. Cain, ed. *Public Policy: The Essential Readings*. Englewood Cliffs, NJ: Prentice Hall, 1995.

Tong, Rosemarie. *Ethics in Policy Analysis*. Englewood Cliffs, NJ: Prentice-Hall, 1986.

Weimer, David L., and Aidan R. Vining. *Policy Analysis: Concepts and Practice*, 3d ed. Upper Saddle River, NJ: Prentice Hall, 1999.

Wells, Donald T., and Chris R. Hamilton. *The Policy Puzzle: Finding Solutions in the Diverse American System*. Upper Saddle River, NJ: Prentice Hall, 1996.

The
Policy Analyst's
Handbook

1

The Scientific Method, Social Science, and Policy Analysis

1.1 Nested Challenges

Effective policy analysts are effective because they understand the various challenges inherent in the analytic task itself. In an ideal world, analysts would be able to arrive at rational answers to rational questions through a rational process of deliberation and analysis, since *rationality*, or the systematic consideration and selection of logical alternatives in light of carefully applied evaluative criteria, is the policy analyst's major objective. Unfortunately, however, policy analysis almost never plays out in this way. We live in a human and political world, and with it comes a variety of subjective concerns and uncertain conditions that prevent us from ever completely reaching that ideal standard. So although we continually strive as policy analysts to achieve or at least approximate this ideal of objective rationality, human and methodological factors invariably get in the way of at least one of the steps toward that goal. From this perspective, the analytic task can be summarized as three sequential and nested processes, each containing a distinct set of methodological and contextual challenges. Effective policy analysts actively manage these challenges from the outset of their analysis.

The first of the three processes that confront the analyst is the challenge of the *scientific method*. When we speak of the scientific method, we are merely speaking of the goal of identifying important questions, theorizing answers to those questions, and then seeking confirmation of our theories through logical reasoning and objective observation. The basic goal of the scientific method is *empirical analysis*, or the establishment of facts determined by the gathering of information through one or more of the five senses. Because policy analysts, like professionals in other fields, view the world through the lenses of preconceived notions about how the world works, they find the scientific method to be particularly challenging.

Put another way, we all carry preconceived beliefs, ideological and otherwise, that tend to shape the ways in which we perceive the world. In some cases and for some analysts, maybe more often than not, preconceptions about "right" and "wrong" turn out to be the correct answers to our important questions as we make policy decisions. But when we fail to subject our assumptions about the world to the scrutiny afforded by a rigorous application of the scientific method, we run the risk of carrying faulty logic or misconceptions throughout our whole problem-solving effort. This failure results in incorrect or incomplete policy recommendations, often with dire and far-reaching consequences. In France during World War II, the failure of the Maginot Line, which led to the occupation of France by Germany, serves as an extreme example of the potentially catastrophic effect of untested and faulty assumptions. Based on outdated data, the French leadership's assumptions regarding German intentions and capabilities caused a misallocation of resources and led to disastrous failure when intelligent and well-intentioned people assumed that things would work as they always had. For policy analysts, the application of the scientific method means always examining and reassessing your basic assumptions and basing one's analysis on empirical evidence whenever possible.

The second process that makes the task of policy analysis challenging is the application of the scientific method to social science questions. When we speak of the *social sciences*, we are speaking of all fields of scholarship and policy that deal with human behavior and human interactions in society. Almost every policy question includes one or more human elements, and thus the special challenges associated with social scientific inquiry almost invariably apply to policy analyses. The basic goals of social science include empirical analysis and the establishment of facts and the validation of theories, but social scientists also often engage in *normative analysis* as part of their research efforts. Normative analysis is value-laden analysis that seeks to assess whether some phenomenon is "good" or "bad." This variety of analysis comes with its own inherent challenges, a topic discussed elsewhere in this book. In general, the special challenge of the application of the scientific method to questions of social science is that human factors, behaviors, and responses are inherently complex and often difficult to measure accurately. Our efforts at wholly rational analysis are almost always bounded by the characteristics of *uncertainty* of measurement and the complexity of human phenomena, meaning that even in the best case we can never hope to get it right all of the time.

As if these challenges were not enough, the policy analyst faces one more set of challenges in his or her bid to achieve objective rationality. Nested within the application of the scientific method to social science is the third process of policy analysis itself. Policy analysis is a special case of social science in that this endeavor comes with its own distinctive methodological and contextual constraints. Every policy analyst operates within a context of practical and political challenges that further limit him in the pursuit of objective and rational solutions to policy problems. These challenges include a wide range of considerations such as decision makers' boundaries, time and resource constraints, prior policy commitments, and other aspects of the policy environment and the context in which decisions will be made. We will address the particulars of these and other constraints in more detail in subsequent sections of the book. To make the task of policy analysis even more challenging, these constraints and the decision-making context frequently change at least once, even after the analyst has begun the analytic process.

Nevertheless, effective policy analysts are effective because they understand and confront these inherent and nested challenges at the outset of the analytic task. Policy analysis is hard to do well because to be successful, the analyst has to deal squarely with all three of these sequential sets of challenges, each step of which can prove fatal if ignored. When things go wrong or if the recommendation proves faulty, analytical shortcomings can usually be traced back to one of these three potential problem areas. The challenge is to anticipate and account for potential problems before beginning each successive step of the problem-solving methodology.

In sum, the policy analyst has to confront the challenges posed by the scientific method, the additional hazards of that method as it is applied to social scientific questions, and the final and critical constraints and challenges specific to policy analysis itself. In order to perform effective policy analysis, we have to understand these challenges and likely limitations of our analytic task from the beginning. Therefore, effective policy analysis must be grounded in an understanding of all three distinctive sets of challenges that face the problem solver. They are considerations that the effective policy analyst always keeps in the back of his or her mind while working through a problem. These distinctive challenges are a large part of the reason that the process of policy analysis is often iterative rather than simply sequential in its application. In the next few sections, we will examine in detail each one of the three nested processes and the related challenges that each process poses for the analyst.

1.2 The Scientific Method

As noted previously, when we speak of the scientific method we are referring to the goal of identifying important questions and then answering those questions as best we can through careful theorizing and objective observation. The effective policy analyst understands that this process is best described as a method that proceeds logically from the characterization of the problem at hand to the identification and collection of information needed to evaluate the problem. The analyst also understands that the scientific method, applied correctly, provides for the crafting of a problem-solving plan of action that will allow him to gather the data needed to analyze the problem at hand efficiently and effectively. There are always time constraints in the world of policy analysis.

Figure 1.1 captures the scientific method in greater detail, and the research pyramid that it contains offers an easy way to visualize the scientific method as a six-step process. Each level of the pyramid represents a level of the process, and we work our way down those levels for the first three steps of the operation, then work our way back to the top of the pyramid for the last three steps. In order, the steps are as follows:

Step 1: Formulate Your Theory

In the first of the six steps of the scientific method, we formulate our theory, in essence defining the nature of our research question or policy problem. In this initial and consequential step of the process, we draw upon our own reason, experience, and judgment as well as other research in formulating a statement of our expectations. Our *theory* can be a relatively abstract statement about how some aspect of the world works, a hunch about a relationship between various phenomena that occur in nature or society, or even merely a statement of our area of analytical interest. It is during this step of the process that we draw upon any previous work done by others to find out what is and is not known about our particular question or hunch. In the research process viewed generally, it is during this step that we decide whether we will aim to extend or challenge the findings of the previous scholarship. The policy analyst uses this preliminary examination of the evidence to begin to structure the problem and to begin to identify the existing empirical evidence that will shape our eventual policy alternatives and the evaluative criteria that we will use to assess them.

Step 2: Operationalize the Theory

Once we have formulated our theory, the next step in the scientific method is to *operationalize* it. We operationalize our relatively

Figure 1.1 **The Research Pyramid**

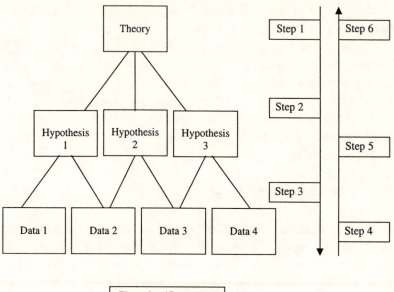

abstract theory when we turn it into a set of concrete, measurable, and testable *hypotheses*. As Figure 1.1 shows, ideally we aim to create a set of hypotheses rather than only one hypothesis, as the usual problems with uncertainty make it better to have multiple tests of our theory's validity rather than only one. During the process of operationalization, we also identify our *independent* and *dependent* variables. As these names suggest, if we believe that two variables are related in some way, we are also likely to believe that we can use one variable to predict changes in the other; the dependent variable is the one whose value depends upon the value

Figure 1.2 **A Hypothesis in Graphic Form**

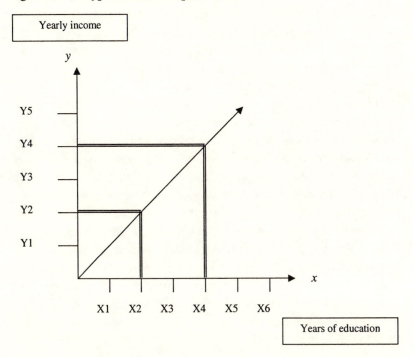

of the other variable. We call that other variable the independent variable because we believe it to be varying freely, at least in the sense that its value is independent of the dependent variable's value.

When we hypothesize these types of relationships between variables, it is usually helpful to graph the relationship. Figure 1.2 shows an example of such a relationship. As we can see in Figure 1.2, this analyst has a theory that there is a relationship between a person's level of education and his overall wealth. The analyst has operationalized that theory into a set of testable hypotheses. One of those hypotheses is described graphically in Figure 1.2, as the analyst believes that we will find a *positive correlation* between the variables "years of education" (the independent variable) and "yearly income" (the dependent variable). That is, this analyst expects that if we were to plot various people's educational attainment measured in years versus their respective amounts of annual income, we would find that as the education increased, the income would increase at the same time. This means that on the graph, X4 is greater than X2, and we expect that Y4 is also greater than Y2 in a positive correlation. Conversely, in a *negative correlation* the value of the dependent variable decreases as the value of the independent variable increases.

It is also important to note that we may or may not believe that the changes in our independent variable actually cause the corresponding changes in the dependent variable. In some cases, we may theorize *causality*, or a cause and effect relationship, but in other cases we may merely see a *correlation*, or a statistical relationship. In *spurious relationships* there is a statistical relationship between two variables but that relationship is purely coincidental.

During this second step of the six-step research process, it is critical that we carefully sort out these issues while defining our key terms and translating our theory into concrete, measurable, and testable hypotheses. The policy analyst has a distinctive set of tasks to accomplish during this phase of policy analysis, tasks that are critical to the success of the analysis. These tasks are described in detail in subsequent chapters.

Step 3: Select Appropriate Research Techniques

Once we have decided on the variables we will use to test our theory, the next step of the scientific method is to determine what data we will use to measure those variables, as well as the means that we will use to gather the data. As Figure 1.1 shows, we will need to identify data to be collected for all of our hypotheses, although some of the hypotheses might rely upon the same data for measuring either the dependent or independent variables. Our basic goal here is to select types of data and collection techniques that will allow us to make *generalizations* about the broader theory that we are aiming to test. We want to select data and collection techniques that avoid giving us results that are *sample specific*, or pertain only to the particular data that we have collected.

Additionally, there are four important research design concerns that we will need to consider during this phase of the application of the scientific method. First, we want to make sure that our variables and the data that we will use to measure them are *appropriate* to our hypothesis. Appropriateness refers to the question of whether or not we are actually measuring the characteristic, quality, or feature that we set out to measure. For example, if we aimed to measure yearly income, but selected a technique of data collection that ignored the income a person received from interest on investments and other income outside of wages, we would be measuring wages rather than yearly income. This shift in our variable might have significant consequences for the validity of the generalizations that we would make after completing our analysis, even though the difference might seem relatively minor when viewed from a broader perspective.

We also want to ensure that our data and collection techniques are *feasible*. That is, it does not help us to identify the best measure of yearly income possible if there are no means of accurately gathering the needed information. For example, we might decide that the best way of measuring yearly income would be to examine the income tax returns of all of the residents of a particular town. Even though the income tax returns would provide us with a solid (though not perfect) measurement of yearly income, this measure is not a feasible one. It is not feasible because we are unlikely to gain access to that personal information, and even if we did have that access, it is unlikely that we would have the time to look at every person's return in even a modest sized town.

A third important research design consideration involves potential *biases* in our data and data collection methods. *Bias* refers to any systematic skew in the way that we measure our variable of interest. For example, if we were to measure the average income in a town through questions asked in a telephone survey, we would bias our estimate of average income upward due to the fact that we would be excluding from our survey all of those citizens without telephones. The term bias refers to any non-random errors that we make as a result of our choice of data collection methods. The fourth aspect of design that we are concerned with is the possibility of other *measurement errors*, or random errors in our measurement of the variables of interest to our study. In general, we would like to select data and data collection techniques that enable us to achieve *efficient estimates* of our variable values. An efficient estimating technique is one that gives us a good chance of achieving estimates close to the true value of the variable of interest, even if we take a relatively small sample from the whole population in which we are interested.

Step 4: Observe Behavior/Collect Data

After we have completed our research design, having selected the appropriate research techniques, we begin the fourth step of the process and execute the research action plan. As we begin our data collection efforts, which may or may not include the observation of specific behaviors, we aim to avoid introducing any biases or measurement errors into those efforts. It is important to note that while we have worked hard to this point to create a research design that precludes or manages potential sources of bias and random measurement errors, we understand that we cannot foresee everything that will take place once we actually begin our data collection. With this in mind, we have to remain vigilant even as we execute the plan, identifying and managing unanticipated sources of bias or measurement error and adapting our collection strategies as necessary as the plan unfolds.

Step 5: Analyze the Data

Once we have gathered our data, we begin to work our way back up the research pyramid, evaluating each of our hypotheses in light of the data that we have collected. During this step in the process, we also ask ourselves whether or not we believe in the data that we have collected, now that we have it. In other words, now that we have gathered the information that we thought we needed, we ask ourselves whether we find those data to be compelling and persuasive. What do the data tell us?

Step 6: Interpret the Results

Once we are convinced of the validity of our data and the implications of those data for our hypotheses, we return to the top of our research pyramid by interpreting our results. In this sixth and final step we use our data and hypotheses to comment on the validity of our theory. Did we confirm what we thought in the first place? Or did we discover that the evidence does not support our theory? Did we accomplish what we set out to do? At this stage in our research effort, we also consider how we might use the knowledge we have gained, and we ask ourselves what the implications of our findings might be. As we will see later in our examination of this process applied specifically to the task of policy analysis, it is also important that we now ask ourselves exactly how we will articulate our results.

1.3   Social Science and the Challenge of Uncertainty

While the application of the scientific method presents its own challenges to the policy analyst seeking to achieve objective and rational analytic results, the fact that we generally operate in the realm of social science adds additional challenges to that mix. The application of the scientific method to the social sciences is often more difficult than the application of that method to the physical sciences owing to the challenge of uncertainty. *Uncertainty* is a general term that refers to all of the potential difficulties that social scientists experience in defining and measuring variables of interest to our various research endeavors. For example, if a chemist decides to measure a quantity of some substance, such as the metal iron, he can do so with relative ease. He selects an arbitrarily defined unit such as a gram, specifies the conditions of temperature and pressure under which the measurement will take place, and measures the amount of the substance that he is examining. This measurement is uncontroversial, as other chemists would agree that this chemist had measured so many units of the substance and that the substance was iron.

On the other hand, consider the task that faces the political scientist aiming to measure a person's political partisanship. What unit of measurement does she use? How does she gather the data or take the measurement? She can define a "Democrat" in any number of ways including party registration, voting behaviors, other forms of political participation, and public policy attitudes. Furthermore, if she decides to use voting behaviors as the means through which she will measure political partisanship, how will she get access to that information? If she decides to conduct a sample survey to gather information on people's voting histories, there are numerous ways that her data can be biased or measured incorrectly. For example, people might forget who they actually voted for some time ago, or they might misrepresent their voting records. Furthermore, some types of people might be more likely than others to respond to this kind of request for personal information, and this political scientist might find her results to be biased for that reason. Finally, after she had collected her data, it would be likely that other political scientists might want to challenge those findings, arguing that other methods of defining "political partisanship" or collecting the data were more appropriate than those she selected. These uncertainties all combine to make investigations in the social sciences harder to conduct well than those in the physical sciences in terms of basic research design, and this uncertainty also means that we are generally less confident of the universal applicability of our findings when we have finished our research effort.

To be more precise on this point, the social scientist faces the challenge of uncertainty at every step of the six-step research process. Social science is concerned with the study of human behaviors, interactions, and societies, and this focus on all things human has inherent complexity and a measure of arbitrariness that colors our research effort from the start. As we formulate our theory, we find that it is often difficult to isolate, even theoretically, the likely causes of some human event, reaction, or tendency. Human nature and human interactions are so complex that it is a distinct challenge to sort through the logic we use to establish our basis for investigation. This challenge of uncertainty becomes even more pronounced as we begin to operationalize our rather abstract theory into workable hypotheses.

Returning to the example of the theorized relationship between "education" and "wealth" that we considered earlier, we find that the challenges of uncertainty inherent in the application of the scientific method to social scientific questions are readily apparent. First, while a social scientist might believe that education does in fact help to determine a person's wealth, no social scientist would claim that education was the only factor determining that wealth. So from the outset of our research, into the relatively broad and abstract notion that there is a relationship between a person's education and his or her overall wealth, the social scientist must admit from the start that there are numerous other variables at work that will influence the relationship that we seek to assess.

Furthermore, the process does not get any easier as we operationalize the theory. As we seek to turn the abstract notions of "education" and "wealth" into more concrete and measurable variables that we can use to create testable hypotheses, we run into more sources of uncertainty as we go along. For example, we might use years of education to measure education and yearly income to measure overall wealth, as suggested in Figure 1.2. However, we would quickly find inadequacies in those measures that might cause problems for us later on when we sought to make generalizations about our findings after gathering the necessary data.

One such potential problem would be found in the use of years of education to measure education in general. While it would be a relatively easy matter to measure a person's number of years of education on a numeric scale, we must also acknowledge that not all years of education are comparable. Some schools are better than others, some students work harder than others during a calendar year, and some types of postsecondary educational experiences could be expected to have a greater impact upon earning potential than others. So while the variable "years of education" could be expected to capture certain aspects of the larger concept "education," we can also see that this measure falls short in several other respects at the same time. Again, this shortcoming falls under the umbrella of the larger idea of uncertainty, and the task that confronts us as social scientists (and policy analysts) is to manage the sources of uncertainty as best we can, understanding that we will never be able to eliminate the potential problem completely. In fact, after carefully considering the alternatives, the researcher might conclude that despite the measure's shortcomings, "years of education" is the most appropriate, feasible, unbiased, and best-measured variable that can be used to get at the larger concept of "education" given the constraints at hand.

As we can see, the same kinds of argument would probably surround the use of yearly income as a measure of overall wealth as well, though we might have even more misgivings about that particular variable. Furthermore, other similar challenges would await us as we next selected the mechanisms through which we would gather our data. Typical methods of data collection in the social sciences include personal and telephonic interviewing, surveys, direct (or participant) observation, primary and secondary document or dataset analysis, and other related means. Each of these methods of data collection comes with its own set of methodological advantages and disadvantages in terms of potential biases, measurement errors, and other plausible sources of uncertainty. The social science researcher is well advised to spend a considerable amount of time in thinking through these and other methodological challenges in advance of any serious data collection or even in advance of a preliminary gathering of relevant evidence. Time spent thinking through these challenges at the outset is usually repaid handsomely in time saved later on in the project and leads to greater validity in the results. Careful research design is the key source of efficiency in any research endeavor, and this is unquestionably true in social science research, given the particular challenges of uncertainty that the social scientist must confront and manage.

1.4 Empirical Analysis and Normative Concerns

Before we turn our attention fully to the specific task of policy analysis, it is appropriate to elaborate a bit upon the distinction between *empirical* and *normative analysis.* Simply put, empirical analysis deals with questions of "is," while normative analysis addresses questions of "ought." In a very real sense, normative concerns add to the nested challenges of the task facing the policy analyst. While physical scientists certainly do not wholly disregard normative concerns or questions of "right" and "wrong" in applying the scientific method in their research endeavors, these normative considerations are frequently secondary at best. That is, one major goal of the scientific method is to separate opinions, hunches, and personal beliefs from the pursuit of substantive truths about the ways that nature works. Therefore, while normative concerns clearly have a place in the physical scientist's endeavors, these concerns are generally relegated to the position of second-order questions. Physical scientists search for "truth," and the normative implications of that truth are considered after its empirical revelations.

Social scientists, however, and the policy analyst as one of those social scientists, even if they share the physical scientists' goal of separating normative concerns from the scientific enterprise, find that normative concerns are inextricably mixed up in the questions they investigate. In fact, it is difficult to think of any public policy question debated in the public sphere today that does not have a significant human component. Similarly, most business concerns have incorporated a respect for the human and social consequences of their business activities into their standard operating practices and decision making, whether out of pragmatism, necessity, or a simple desire to do the right thing.

In any event, normative considerations shape the social scientists' application of the scientific method to social science questions in a number of ways. First, normative considerations in policy analysis add a layer of subjectivity to our analysis that is difficult to avoid, if it can be avoided at all. This subjectivity comes from the basic premise that values are exactly that—subjective interpretations of what is an acceptable behavior or attitude, and what is not. Therefore, not only will the policy analyst almost necessarily bring to bear his or her own values to any policy analysis, but that analyst is also likely to run into at least modest differences in values among the other participants in the analytic task. The normative components of the policy analysis that serve as the basis for a policy recommendation may be agreed upon by members of one organization, only to be rejected or seriously questioned by members of another. This subjectivity inherent in normative considerations can also take the form of constraints upon potential courses of action that will prevent us from approaching the objective rationality that we strive to achieve.

Likewise, normative concerns almost always include additional sources of uncertainty (for example, additional issue complexity and difficulty of qualification or quantification) that can obscure the analytic task. By their very nature, normative concerns are difficult to define and measure, a characteristic that has significant consequences when we try to impose a rational and ordered method of criterion assessment upon competing potential courses of action. As we look further into the specific techniques of policy analysis, it will be apparent that the additional challenges that the normative components of our analysis present should not be underestimated and that they are challenges that must be confronted squarely by the policy analyst throughout the analysis.

None of these points regarding the role of normative analysis should be construed as aiming at diminishing the role or importance or of normative considerations in policy analysis and other social scientific research endeavors. On the contrary, it is these normative concerns that make the analytic task as critical as it is. There are human consequences to the choices and recommendations that we make in the course of our analysis. The inevitability of these consequences makes it especially important that we understand the nature of the challenges that the social scientist must confront, so that we take the proper steps to give ourselves the best chance possible of arriving at the "right" answers. More often than not, the normative considerations asserted or implied by the social scientist's theory formulation are in fact the first-order questions of most importance to us all.

1.5 The Goals of Policy Analysis

The ultimate goal of the policy analyst is to achieve objective ra- *wrong!* tionality in the consideration of important issues, but in a sense this goal represents the Holy Grail of the analytical world. That is, effective policy analysts continually strive to achieve this standard, even as they know full well that they can never quite get there given the limits inherent in the analytic task. Nevertheless, *objective rationality* is the goal, and this term refers to analysis based upon careful reasoning, logic, and empirical observation that is uninfluenced by emotion, predispositions, and personal preferences. This is not to say that hunches, experience, and intuition cannot be right on occasion or that they contribute nothing to the analysis, but rather that no assumption should remain untested, or at least unconsidered, during the process of objective rational analysis. The point here is that we strive to approximate objective rationality, even when we know that we can never wholly eliminate those considerations that divert us from that standard.

In addition to this overarching goal, which shapes the effective analyst's approach to problem solving in the first place, the analyst also usually has another related objective in mind from the outset of the analytical effort. Generally speaking, policy analysts are either interested in finding the most efficient solution to their problems, one that maximizes a particular criterion value, or they are alternately intent upon finding a solution that achieves the optimal combination of a number of specified criteria of interest to them. To put this in practical terms, analysts concerned with *efficiency* are usually interested in finding a solution to their issue that maximizes the net benefit to be realized from a policy change, with this net benefit most often measured in dollars. In the second case, the analyst concerned with achieving *optimality* is interested in identifying the solution that offers the most desirable mix of values among a set of criteria. These criteria can include anything of importance to the analyst, including normative considerations, and the various criteria can be weighted in importance in any way deemed appropriate by the analyst.

These alternative objectives correspond to the two most prevalent methods of policy analysis. *Cost-benefit analysis* (CBA) allows the analyst concerned with achieving efficiency in terms of net costs and benefits to consider alternatives in light of this criterion in a structured way. CBA involves the careful identification and quantification of all of the costs and benefits associated with potential policy changes. Competing potential courses of action, including the status quo, are then compared with one another on the basis of projected net costs or benefits. The alternative that offers the greatest likely net benefit is the option that is recommended to the decision maker.

For those analysts interested in identifying the optimal mix among a set of utilitarian and normative criteria, *multi-attribute analysis* (MAA) is the appropriate analytical technique. MAA allows the analyst to identify the policy alternative in a set of potential courses of action that will offer the most attractive combination or best balance among a set of consequential criteria. In the application of this technique, competing potential courses of action, again including the status quo, are evaluated in accordance with the various selected criteria. The criteria values for each course of action are then translated to a common scale, with the various criteria weighted in terms of their relative importance. Each potential course of action receives an overall score, and the alternative with the best overall score becomes the recommended alternative.

Given the usual uncertainties associated with many issues, the calculated net benefits and the multi-attribute scores may in fact be represented as the expected values of a set of probabilities. Furthermore, in the application of each of the methods of policy analysis, the critical assumptions that shape the analytical logic are examined carefully to determine whether the results are sensitive to change. These methods of analysis, each examined in detail in later chapters, represent the formal ways in which policy analysts seek to solve policy problems by approximating objective rationality as well as possible.

1.6 The Limits of Rationality

A number of factors inherent in the process of policy analysis prevent us from attaining the objective rationality that we set out to achieve. As noted in previous sections, the scientific method itself comes with distinct challenges in terms of our ability to carry out empirical analysis. Even in the best of situations, it is difficult to define our theories and hypotheses precisely, and it is similarly difficult to find data that are wholly appropriate to the variables and concepts that we seek to measure. Furthermore, the application of the scientific method to social science questions adds an additional layer of uncertainty and difficulty to our research efforts given the challenges of measurement and the arbitrariness and complexity of human behaviors in the first place. The research enterprise would be difficult enough if these were the only challenges that we faced in the pursuit of objective rationality.

However, our bid for this ideal standard is further limited by additional challenges inherent in the analytic task itself. The two most important additional challenges that policy analysts face are those of *prediction* and *particularity*. In general, social scientists aim to accomplish three distinct goals at different times. Sometimes social scientists attempt to *explain* various human phenomena or human events, that is, they examine a mass of information pertaining to a phenomenon or event with the goal of identifying the most important facts regarding an aspect of that characteristic or event. An example of this goal is provided by the historian who attempts to explain the rationale behind a nation's decision to go to war. A second goal of the social scientist is to *describe* human characteristics or a human event. In this instance, the social scientist uses a limited amount of information, and extrapolates from the limited known information to tell us more than we knew before about a characteristic or event. An example of this research endeavor is the political scientist who conducts a limited exit poll during a state election but uses the information gathered to make broad generalizations about what it was that caused the entire electorate of the state to vote the way they did.

The third, and most challenging, goal of the social scientist, however, is to predict future human events or the implications of changes in the human condition, social relationships, or social arrangements. When the social scientist offers a *prediction*, this means that the social scientist is taking a limited amount of information and projecting future events and outcomes. The idea here is that regardless of the amount of information available to the social scientist, the uncertainty and complexity inherent in social science endeavors means that at best we can provide probabilities in our predictions, but not guarantees. Even worse, in the realm of policy analysis, it is probable that we will not be able to account for everything that is likely to occur once a policy change is implemented. Policy analysts call this usual unanticipated variance from predicted outcomes "the law of unintended consequences." Effective policy analysts understand the limits of rationality from this perspective. Things will never turn out exactly the way that we expect.

The second direct challenge to objective rationality that the policy analyst faces to a greater extent than other social scientists is the challenge presented by the *particularity* of the usual policy problem. *Particularity* refers to the fact that most policy problems and their potential solutions are specific to a particular context. More than most social science endeavors, policy analysis does not lend itself readily to out-of-sample generalization. As an example, if the city of Atlanta changes its policy of binding arbitration that defines its negotiating relationship with its firefighters and police officers, it does not necessarily follow that comparably sized Pittsburgh will realize the same effects if it makes a similar change. Some of the consequences of the change in Atlanta will be different from the implications of the change for Pittsburgh, owing to variations in political climate, citizen expectations, union reactions, negotiating tactics, and budgetary differences, among other differences. Prediction and particularity challenge the policy analyst in the pursuit of rationality, and they limit the rationality possible in both the process and the product.

1.7   Other Challenges for the Policy Analyst

In addition to the challenges inherent in the social science task itself, there are a number of other contextual challenges that also conspire to prevent the analyst from approaching objective rationality. The first of these additional challenges is ordinary: lack of enough time to carry the analysis through to its logical completion. Deadlines, competing demands for time, and the scope of the analytic task itself limit the analyst's time, and it is unlikely that the analyst will have the luxury of unconstrained time to deliberate on a given policy question except for the most critical of analytic tasks. Analysts almost always end up making hard trade-offs between time and depth of analysis.

Likewise, analysts typically face other resource constraints in their efforts at thorough, rational, and unbiased analysis. They often have to choose methods of data collection that are less effective but also less resource intensive than others in order to get the baseline information upon which they will base their predictions. To explain this constraint another way, policy analysis is usually conducted within a budget, and analysts are frequently limited in the range of data collection methods available to them in their analysis given budgetary constraints. This constraint can involve limits on the purchase of relevant datasets, limits on money available for surveying or telephonic interviewing, or other similar restrictions.

The policy analyst is likely to encounter other roadblocks on the path to rationality as well. Many times, the range of feasible prospective policy changes is limited by prior policy commitments or decisions made in the past in the particular issue area. These prior commitments can limit the range of feasible change in two ways. First, the prior commitments can reduce the number of potential courses of action available to the analyst. Furthermore, the prior commitments can encourage *incrementalism*, or a tendency to implement only modest changes to the existing policies, in the overall approach to change. Decision makers' preferences, political considerations, and other factors serve to reinforce this tendency toward incrementalism in policy making in general and therefore serve as further constraints on the rational analyst's pursuit of objective and reasoned policy recommendations. With all of these caveats in mind, one might wonder why we should bother engaging in formal policy analysis in the first place. We bother because it is the process of formal policy analysis that gives us the best chance of "getting it right," even if our rationality exists only in segments within the boundaries of a political and uncertain world.

1.8   The General Analytical Framework

Although this book outlines two distinct problem-solving methods aimed at two different sets of evaluative criteria, there is a basic analytical framework common to those and other rational approaches to policy analysis. This problem-solving framework proceeds sequentially but is also iterative. That is, even though this method of considering policy problems is intended to proceed in a logical and progressive step-by-step fashion, it is common for the analyst to repeat steps of the process as new information defines and redefines the problem, alternatives, and evaluative criteria. Even so, there is a beginning, middle, and end to the task. In essence, this analytical framework represents the scientific method applied to the particular case of policy analysis.

As Table 1.1 illustrates, there are nine steps in the process viewed generally. The first and possibly most crucial step of the problem-solving process is that of *defining the problem*. During this stage of the process of policy analysis, we conduct our preliminary investigation of the issue area, gather relevant evidence, and define the terms of the issue as precisely as we can. As the problem of definition has critical implications for the shape of all activity that will follow, we will take a much closer look at this process in chapter 2. After we have defined the problem and in the process determined whether a problem actually exists, we turn our attention to *generating potential courses of action*, or COAs. It is important to note from the outset that this is a distinct step in itself, and it is the second rather than first step in the analytical process. More often than not, many analysts and decision makers begin

Table 1.1

The Basic Analytical Framework

Step 1:   Define the problem

Step 2:   Generate potential courses of action (COA)

Step 3:   Identify the potential advantages and disadvantages of each COA

Step 4:   Select the evaluative criteria

Step 5:   Predict the consequences of each COA in terms of the evaluative criteria

Step 6:   Analyze the sensitivity of your critical assumptions and findings

Step 7:   Choose a recommended COA

Step 8:   Articulate your recommendation

Step 9:   Implement, supervise, and assess the results

their analysis as a "yes/no" proposition that revolves around one seemingly desirable potential COA. It is not uncommon for this kind of "analysis" to become an exercise in rationalization in which the "analyst" is instructed to find evidence that will support a particular recommendation. Check with any local legislator's staff if you doubt that this kind of analysis exists. This kind of analytical activity has given rise to the wry expression, "That's a solution in search of a problem."

But for the objective and rational analyst in search of an honest assessment of a policy problem, the generation of potential COAs involves brainstorming, interviewing, primary and secondary document analysis, and other activities. The analyst's goal is to take an open-minded approach to the consideration of potential solutions to a well-defined need. The analyst is careful to generate all of the potential COA prior to beginning to evaluate any of them. The effective analyst understands that COA generation and evaluation are distinct steps in the analytical process. Chapter 3 addresses this process in much more detail.

Once we have generated potential solutions to our well-defined policy problem, we then begin our assessments of each of these potential COAs. We accomplish this initial assessment through a somewhat freeform *identification of the advantages and disadvantages of each COA*. That is, we aim to identify every potential advantage and disadvantage that might be associated with a possible policy change, however large or small and whether empirical or normative in nature. In some cases, we may find that potential disadvantages associated with a COA might even preclude that COA's further consideration, and it is at this point that we would reject that COA as being unfeasible.

As we identify these potential advantages and disadvantages, we also begin to think about the characteristics of any solution to our problem that are likely to be most important to us. We then *select the evaluative criteria* that we will use to formally assess our alternative COAs. It is at this point that we also select an analytic technique, as we most often either focus on the sole criterion of efficiency or seek to achieve optimality among a set of criteria. In chapter 4 we carefully examine the application of cost-benefit analysis as it relates to the pursuit of efficiency, while in chapter 5 we detail the application of the technique of multi-attribute analysis, which enables us to achieve the rational optimality that we might seek. Using these techniques then, we *predict the consequences of each COA in terms of the evaluative criteria*.

These predictions are based on logic, empirical evidence, and probabilities, and we therefore take the additional precaution of *analyzing the sensitivity of our analysis in light of our critical assumptions and assessments*. After that careful analysis of the sensitivity of our assumptions and findings, we *choose a COA* that we will recommend, and we *articulate our findings and recommendation*. Finally, we *implement* our policy change, supervise that implementation to ensure that the decision maker's intent is met, and assess the consequences, both intended and otherwise, of the policy change. In some cases the analyst has a role in the implementation and in some cases not, but in all cases the analyst seeks to learn from that implementation as it certainly affects future policy analysis in that issue area. Chapters 6 and 7 examine some of these special considerations in the final stages of the analytical process.

1.9 Notes and Supplementary Readings

Complete bibliographic entries for the sources listed in this section and in the notes for the succeeding chapters are contained in the bibliography at the end of the book. While this list of works is certainly not an exhaustive compilation of the fine literature in the fields of policy analysis and policy making, taken together these scholarly works are intended to provide insightful, focused, and comprehensive insights into key topics addressed in the associated chapters.

• Scholars and analysts have debated the desirability and feasibility of the pursuit of rationality in policy analysis for many years. S.I. Benn and G.W. Mortimore offer various definitions of "rationality" as commonly employed in the social sciences as well as a classic critique of those applications in their edited volume, *Rationality and the Social Sciences* (1978). The book is a collection of papers by various scholars in the social sciences dealing with the different aspects and implications of rationalism as it pertains to social scientific inquiry. Of particular note is S.I. Benn's chapter 10, "Rationality and Political Behaviour," in which the author gives an effective overview of Anthony Downs's concept of voter "role-rationality." Benn also describes "strong" versus "weak" rationality as they relate to public preferences and participation in political and policy-making events.

• In a parallel vein, Stuart Nagel describes alternative definitions of "rationality" in chapter 1 of *Policy Studies: Integration and Evaluation* (1988), and he addresses the criteria for evaluating the quality of policy studies research in chapter 2 of the book. Among these criteria, he includes usefulness, validity, and importance, and he analyzes the fundamental goals of the criteria selection.

- In *Public Policy Decision Making: Systems Analysis and Comparative Advantages Debate* (1973), Bernard L. Brock, James Chesebro, John Gragus, and James Klumpp, offer a critique of earlier attempts at rational, comprehensive policy analysis in describing the evolution of the decision-making process. In chapter 1, the authors focus on the limits inherent in the "comprehensive rational" approach and on the challenges posed by having policy participants and decision makers involved in the problem solving process. In chapter 2, the authors address the implications of the policy-making environment for the analytic process. The authors describe the characteristics of "closed" versus "open" policy systems and the impact of environmental interaction on the resulting decision-making processes. Subsequent chapters of the book relate these and other concepts to the broader process of policy analysis viewed from a "systems" perspective.

- Morris P. Fiorina and Ian Shapiro debated the validity of rational choice approaches to social science questions in a pair of articles in the *New York Times* on February 26, 2000. Fiorina argued that the rational choice approach has limitations, like other social science models, but that its benefits outweigh its shortcomings. He went on to argue that the model's validity is apparent in most analyses of political outcomes, and he saw the model as being particularly valuable in the high-stakes political choices and the key policy decisions that individual actors and governments make. Shapiro, on the other hand, saw shortfalls in the predictive capabilities of political science models based upon rational choice assumptions. These scholars' exchange is representative of an ongoing debate in much of social science regarding the validity and desirability of rational choice approaches to a variety of questions.

- Catherine Hakim elaborates upon the importance of research design considerations as they apply to social science research generally in chapter 1 of *Research Design: Successful Designs for Social and Economic Research* (2000). She also describes the respective advantages and disadvantages of the various methods of data collection in chapters 4 through 9 of the book, including a look at the challenges of sample surveying in chapter 6.

• Lavinia Mitton, Holly Sutherland, and Melvyn Weeks describe the benefits of "microsimulation models" in policy analysis in chapter 1 of their edited volume, *Microsimulation Modelling for Policy Analysis* (2000). This technique involves the use of micro-level data to glean insights into the effect of policy changes at the individual level. These insights can then be aggregated to offer estimates of the likely overall effect of a potential policy change. The book also addresses in detail the various and significant challenges of prediction that confront the policy analyst in the pursuit of valid estimates.

• Chapter 3 of William N. Dunn's edited volume, *Values, Ethics, and the Practice of Policy Analysis* (1983), examines the role of normative considerations in public policy analysis. In that chapter, Pamela Doty finds that normative concerns are prominent in the majority of policy products obtained from policy-oriented research institutes, regardless of the areas of policy interest. This finding suggests that the cost-benefit analyses and efficiency-based policy evaluations that predominate today may in fact be missing key policy concerns as a result of the reliance on this particular method.

• Stuart Nagel offers a description of rational choice theory and rational choice approaches to policy analysis in chapter 2 of his edited volume, *Improving Policy Analysis* (1980). In chapter 2, John E. Brandl also addresses the fine line between viewing rational choice theory as a descriptive theory and embracing it as a normative standard. Brandl then examines the implications of self-interested behaviors and motives as they relate to the interpretation of policy alternatives. Chapter 4 offers a critique of attempts at purely "rational" analysis, as Jack Byrd Jr. argues that these efforts risk losing the advantages conferred by the judgment, intuition, and experience of the analyst.

• Gary King, Robert O. Keohane, and Sidney Verba analyze the essential features of effective research design in their important book, *Designing Social Inquiry* (1994). The first chapter explores the implications of the application of the scientific method to the social sciences in rigorous detail, and their subsequent chapters examine the concepts of "uncertainty," "bias," "measurement errors," and other design considerations. Additionally, the authors describe the various trade-offs that researchers make in selecting their means of data collection, as well as the various interpretations of the relationships that we theorize in our analysis.

• Charles Lindblom explains the limits on rationality in executive decision making and policy analysis in his article, "The 'Science' of Muddling Through" (1959), as well as his book, *The Policymaking Process* (1980). He describes the "root" method, or a rational-comprehensive approach, as unrealistic, and contrasts this approach with "successive limited comparisons," or a "branch" method. In chapter 3 of the book, Lindblom offers his thoughts on the limits of rational analysis given the usual context of politics in which that analysis occurs.

• In chapter 4 of *Agendas, Alternatives, and Public Policies* (1994), an important book on the policy-making process, John W. Kingdon identifies the natural limits on rational decision making and other factors that shape policy analysis. Additionally, he offers insights into the challenges associated with interview and case-study methodologies in his "Appendix on Methods" in the book. Richard F. Fenno Jr. also provides an important perspective on these and other methodological challenges in his own "Notes on Method: Participant Observation" in *Home Style: House Members in Their Districts* (1978).

• Robert Formaini describes the challenges of uncertainty in the context of risk assessment and probabilities in chapter 1 of *The Myth of Scientific Public Policy* (1990).

• David R. Mayhew provides an excellent example of the rational application of theory leavened with empirical analysis in *Congress: The Electoral Connection* (1974).

• In chapter 1 of Frank Fischer and John Forester's edited volume, *Confronting Values in Policy Analysis* (1987), Charles W. Anderson describes the challenges inherent in reducing public issues from relatively abstract values to specific policy choices. In chapter 2, Douglas J. Amy offers thoughts on the incorporation of ethics into policy questions and policy administration. In chapter 5, Bruce Jennings highlights the difficulties that face the analyst in interpreting the actual effects of existing policies and offers some potential prescriptions for those difficulties. Timothy W. Luke critiques rational choice theory in chapter 7, while Rosemarie Tong describes the particular ethical and political challenges that routinely confront policy analysts and administrators in the execution of their public responsibilities in chapter 8. In chapter 9, Leonard A. Cole elaborates on the ethical limitations on experimentation in social scientific inquiry in his description of the U.S. Army's testing procedures of the 1950s.

• In chapter 2 of *Theoretical Issues in Policy Analysis* (1988), M.E. Hawkesworth critiques the reliance upon empirical methods and rationalism in policy analysis, asserting the existence of a "fact/value dichotomy" that limits the effectiveness and desirability of those methods.

• In chapter 6 of Frank P. Scioli Jr. and Thomas J. Cook's *Methodologies for Analyzing Public Policies* (1975), Donald S. Van Meter and Herbert B. Asher offer a cautionary note regarding the limitations on the specification of cause and effect relationships in public policy analyses. At the same time, the authors argue for the need for theorizing causality in order to generate meaningful analytic designs. Van Meter and Asher also offer examples of partial and complete models of student performance to illustrate the importance of this step in the analytical process.

• Chapter 1 of Duncan MacRae Jr. and James A. Wilde's *Policy Analysis for Public Decisions* (1985) provides an alternative perspective on the elements of a successful policy analysis. This chapter also includes a brief glossary in which the authors outline some of the terms commonly found in the field of policy analysis.

• Randall S. Clemons and Mark K. McBeth offer a critique of the "rational public policy method" in chapter 2 of *Public Policy Praxis* (2001), and they comment on the difficulties of prediction inherent in the task of policy analysis. The authors go on in chapter 4 to give an overview of Kingdon's model of the public agenda setting process, offering that process as an alternative to rational formalism. Clemons and McBeth offer a variety of mini cases in support of their perspectives on policy making and analysis.

• Michael Corbett provides an alternative perspective on social scientific research methods along with an introduction to the MicroCase statistical software package in *Research Methods in Political Science* (2001).

• In chapter 1 of Stella A. Theodoulou and Matthew A. Cain's *Public Policy: The Essential Readings* (1995), Theodoulou differentiates between the "politics" and "policy" of public policy analysis. She also introduces a variety of theoretical perspectives on the policy-making process, including group theory, elite theory, corporatism, and the theory of subgovernments. In chapter 2 of the book, Paul Sabatier traces the development of public policy studies as a subset of American political science.

• Charles F. Bonser, Eugene B. McGregor Jr., and Clinton V. Oster Jr. outline the history of the development of regulatory policies in American government in chapter 4 of *American Public Policy Problems* (2000).

• B. Guy Peters elaborates upon the wide variety of issues and forms of regulations encompassed by the term "public policy" in chapter 1 of *American Public Policy: Promise and Performance* (2000).

• Frank Fischer elaborates upon the challenges of integrating empirical analysis and normative concerns in chapter 1 of his book, *Evaluating Public Policy* (1995). Fischer goes on to offer a frame-

work with which the analyst can place the evaluative criteria selected into the context of the organizational situation. In chapter 9
of the book, Fischer provides insight into the particular constraints
and challenges that correspond to the consideration of environmental policy changes.

• Deborah Stone describes the shortcomings of efficiency-based
techniques of policy analysis as they relate to normative considerations in *Policy Paradox: The Art of Political Decision Making*
(1997). In chapter 2 of her book, the author examines the often-
conflicting policy goals of equity, efficiency, security, and liberty.

• J. Johnston's *Econometric Methods* (1984) provides a detailed
explication of the mathematics underlying applied econometrics.
Peter Kennedy's *A Guide to Econometrics* (1998) offers similar
rigor in its treatment of the subject of econometrics, but this text
approaches the subject in a manner that will be more accessible to
those with less grounding in mathematics.

• Stephen Van Evera's *Guide to Methods for Students of Political Science* (1997) offers an alternative explanation of the fundamental principles of social science research methodology applied
to political questions. Chapter 2 of his book outlines an effective
approach to case study selection as well as guidelines for knowing
when the case study approach is an appropriate research technique.

• Fritz W. Scharpf explains rational choice applications and
game theory in the analysis of institutions in *Games Real Actors
Play: Actor-Centered Institutionalism in Policy Research* (1997).

• Chapter 1 of Kenneth A. Shepsle and Mark S. Bonchek's *Analyzing Politics: Rationality, Behavior, and Institutions* (1997) describes the evolution of goals within the field of political science
over the last century. This chapter also offers an alternative perspective on the use of models and the assumption of rationality as
they are applied in the discipline today.

• Chava Frankfort-Nachmias and David Nachmias present a thorough treatment of the various steps of the scientific method applied to human questions in *Research Methods in the Social Sciences*, 6th edition (2000). The chapters of this book survey the scientific method, research design, various data collection techniques, and the interpretation of the results. The book also includes an introduction to the SPSS statistical software package (SPSS, Inc.).

2

Defining the Problem

2.1 The Problem Definition

In many respects, the first step of the analytical process is the most critical one, paving the way to eventual success or misdirecting our efforts from the outset. The problem definition, when done well, not only identifies the issue to be examined in precise, coherent, and complete terms, but also suggests a tentative research agenda and plan of action for our subsequent data collection. Effective policy analysts understand that a precise problem definition is their best labor saving device, and therefore, at the start of the task skillful analysts spend a good deal of the time available to them thinking through the parameters of their problems. The problem definition sets the tone for all of the analysis that will follow, and it is generally true that analysts who take the time to work through definitional issues up front are rewarded with subsequent analytical success. Precise problem definitions serve as the blueprint for that analytical success.

The easiest (and perhaps most appropriate) analogy to make in demonstrating the benefits of time spent in defining the problem is that of two students facing the prospect of writing a paper for the same class. One student immediately rushes to the library and checks out every book he can on his particular topic, after which he begins to work his way haphazardly from book to book hoping he will stumble across something relevant to his paper topic. The paper that results from this effort is a mishmash of ideas and evidence with holes in both, and it is graded accordingly. Conversely, the other student spends some time thinking through the paper topic and some potential arguments she might make, as well as the kinds of evidence that might be relevant to this problem. The next day, she walks calmly into the library, finds the three books she thought she might need, and is pleased to find that they do in fact have the exact evidence she needs to make a coherent and rational argument. She quickly writes a focused, logical, and successful paper in half the time that it took the other student to write his paper, with far better results in terms of quality and economy of effort. In much the same way, effective policy analysts use the process of careful problem definition to realize potential efficiencies and to improve the products that result from focused and logical approaches to the analyses.

The task of problem definition requires a careful consideration of the parameters of an issue and the context within which a recommendation for a policy change will be made. As in the corresponding first step of the scientific method, the impetus for the problem to be defined can come from anywhere. But regardless of whether the incentive is the decision maker's guidance, your own need for a decision, or something else that is driving the analysis, this step affords us the opportunity to think through the problem in an unconstrained and rational way before we incorporate the inevitable arbitrary limits on the process. At the same time, problem definition forces us to think about what it is that we are really concerned about as we embark on the analytical task, and it forces us to focus our research effort. Without question, any time spent thinking through the problem at hand at the outset is invariably repaid with interest later in the process. Put another way, sometimes it is more important to stare at the ceiling and think for a while than to spring into a flurry of misdirected action, even when we are confronted with a short-notice, short-suspense requirement. Effective policy analysts understand the vital importance of precise problem definitions.

2.2 Is There Really a Problem?

The first question every analyst should ask is whether a legitimate problem exists. This question seems very basic, but it is frequently ignored in the rush to justify favored solutions to perceived problems. In asking the question, the analyst not only seeks to find out whether there is a problem, but also what the magnitude and essence of that problem might be. In this preliminary search for specific evidence of the alleged problem, the analyst seeks an empirical confirmation of the issue, aiming to identify the scope of the problem as it relates to the context in which any policy change might be made. After this preliminary data collection effort, the analyst should be able to quantify or at least qualify the nature of the problem in straightforward terms.

This first step in the process of defining the problem is often ignored, but it is absolutely critical to the rationality and effectiveness of any problem-solving effort. When we collect empirical evidence to substantiate the existence of a problem, we also begin to structure potential solutions to the problem, and this effort begins the process of identifying the additional evidence that we will need later in the process. It is also at this point that we start to sort our variables, tentatively identifying important factors as independent and dependent variables based upon our preliminary evidence, intuition, theory, and logic. In a sense, it is at this point that we begin to identify the "center of mass" of the problem, and this empirical verification helps us to begin to frame the problem in our minds in a rational way.

To put these ideas into practical terms, consider the following hypothetical example. In a medium-sized city, one of the popular local television newscasts does a series on the plight of homeless people in the city, and the series is critical of the mayor's "lack of action" on the issue. A common response to a situation of this type would be for the mayor to direct his staff to "get something done about the homeless people and get it done fast, and I want the police involved." The staff then turns its attention to the city budget to find dollars to make available to city relief agencies, and they might direct the police department or other public safety officials to be proactive in offering support and assistance to any homeless people they find on the streets. Two days later, the exhausted staff members stand by wearily as the mayor announces in a press conference that "these measures have been taken to ensure that our city does not ignore the plight of its least fortunate citizens." Six months later, nothing has changed except that the police department has one more vaguely defined responsibility while the city has provided vital funds that are sitting unused or were squandered on services that had little relevance to the actual problem at hand.

Some relevant "Do we have a problem?" questions might have helped a great deal in this case. First, how many homeless people does the city have? In general, why are these people homeless? If given alternatives, will these people use the alternatives, such as subsidized housing, temporary shelters, food vouchers, or the like? Is mental health an issue here? What have other cities done to deal with the problem, and how successful have their efforts been? What do the people who run the city's relief agencies think about the problem? In their experience, what has worked in the past and what has not? How would they use any additional funds that became available? What research on the subject is available, and what do the various advocacy groups have to say on the subject? A modest amount of data collection at the outset goes a long way toward programming the problem solvers for eventual success in addressing a situation such as this one. Again, the question of whether or not a problem exists in the first place seems very basic, but it is frequently ignored in the rush to "get something done." We then revisit the problem in the future having squandered resources that could have been used to help fix the real underlying problems in the first place.

2.3 An Iterative Process

From the beginning, the process of policy analysis is iterative as much as it is sequential. That is, while the analytic process does proceed in a logical way, it is often the case that we revisit steps in the process as new information comes to light. Therefore, while the first step in the analytical process involves carefully defining the problem in light of a preliminary check of some relevant evidence, we expect that our subsequent data collection efforts will in fact refine that problem definition further. The same can be said of the other steps in the analytical process and for the process viewed as a whole as well. When we reach the last step in the process, that of implementing, supervising, and assessing the results, in a fashion we have just begun the problem definition for another policy problem. Policy analysis is quite often circular and iterative in this sense, and we should be prepared from the beginning to revise our assumptions or extend our evidence, backtracking as necessary as we work through the problem at hand.

2.4 Thinking Ahead to the Analytic Technique

Just as the process of policy analysis is iterative, it is also forward looking. That is, as we develop our precise definition of the policy problem in light of our initial data collection efforts, we also begin to think ahead to the analytic method that we will use later in the project. Thinking along these lines from the start enables us to visualize an effective analytical plan of action and to economize on effort. Therefore, during the problem definition stage of the process we not only gather evidence that pertains to the issue in question, but we also identify critical parameters and objectives that will shape our solution. As part of this effort, the analyst seeks out formal and informal guidance regarding the parameters and objectives that any problem solution will have to incorporate within it. Constraints, parameters, and objectives come from the decision makers, public statutes, organizational standard operating procedures, and other such sources. Put another way, during problem definition we not only look at substantive evidence that tells us about the existence, scope, and magnitude of our policy problem, but we also look at the context in which we will solve the problem. Both types of information are critical as we aim to define our particular problem precisely, and early on in the process we will begin to identify key concerns or aspects of the problem that must be addressed in order to bring about the positive changes that we want.

For some issues, achieving the most effective allocation of scarce resources will be the primary goal of the analysis, and for those issues a cost-benefit analysis (CBA) will be most appropriate. For other issues, we may aim to satisfy a number of different considerations as best we can, balancing our needs in one area against needs in others. For these problems, as well as others that have significant normative considerations as central concerns, multi-attribute analysis (MAA) will eventually be our analytical technique of choice. But it is during the process of defining our problem that we begin to visualize the shape of the broader analytical effort, and this visualization begins to influence our data collection strategies as we get further into the problem-solving process.

2.5 Critical Elements of the Precise Problem Definition

Regardless of the issue, effective and precise problem definitions have a number of features in common. First, they *define the issue clearly and logically, rather than editorially*. The analyst takes a dispassionate view of the issue, aiming from the start to achieve rational and empirical qualities in the analysis. Precise problem definitions also *define the key terms* that relate to a policy problem, and they outline the essence of the problem at hand in terms of the *likely critical explanatory variables* of interest to the investigation. Additionally, we may go further than this by also identifying whether those critical variables are likely to be independent or dependent, based upon our preliminary look at the evidence and our judgment.

Precise problem definitions also include *empirical evidence* that verifies the validity and magnitude of the problem we are analyzing. At the same time, good problem definitions also *identify other data needed* for a thorough investigation of the issue. Effective problem definitions likewise *identify the likely obstacles* to policy change, including natural constraints, political constraints, decision makers' parameters, or other conditions that will limit the range of feasible policy changes in some way. Finally, it is often appropriate in the problem definition to mention a tentative analytical technique that will be applied in the solution of the problem as well as a timeline for the completion of the project, if that is known.

Furthermore, it is always a good idea for the analyst to go through the drill of actually writing a concise and precise definition of the issue at hand after having completed some preliminary data collection and thinking on the problem. The written problem definition forces the analyst to think through the problem and the analytical plan of action, and this written problem definition should be distributed to the decision maker and to those who will assist in the analysis. This dissemination of the problem definition ensures that everyone understands the problem the same way, agrees upon the objectives of the analysis, and concurs on the important parameters that will shape the consideration of alternatives. The resultant feedback that the analyst receives is used to refine both the definition of the problem and the project's research plan of action. It is always better to arrive at consensus on the problem definition at the outset of the analysis than to invest time, energy, and resources going in the wrong direction.

The length of the problem definition will depend upon the scope and magnitude of the problem at hand, but generally speaking the problem definition should be brief. Ordinarily, we will aim to define the problem precisely, coherently, and completely in two or three pages of prose. Since the problem definition is an important part of a decision-making process, we try to keep it concise and direct like the other analytical products to come. Here, as elsewhere, we aim to streamline our prose in order to get the point across clearly and succinctly. In most cases, the decision makers or other consumers of the analytic products will have their own time constraints, so this efficiency will generally work to everyone's advantage.

There is a high return on investment for time spent on this step in the problem-solving process, but only if everyone concerned clearly and correctly understands the analyst's perspective on the problem. It is not uncommon for analysts to assert that the problem definition stage of a project is the most difficult aspect of the analytical task. It requires some critical fact-finding and certainly requires as much or more thinking than other steps in the process. But once the problem definition is done well and agreed upon by the analysts and decision makers, the path to analytic success is fairly clear, and the analyst can spend his most precious resource, time, wisely and well.

2.6 The Policy-making Process and the Problem Definition

Before we leave the topic of precise problem definition and begin to look at the other steps of the analytic process, it is appropriate to spend a moment considering the impact of the policy making process itself on the problem definition. Regardless of the policy area in which it takes place, policy making generally consists of the same four steps. First, a problem of some type is identified, whether as part of a systematic organizational process or as an independent event. Next, the identified problem is considered, and potential solutions are generated. Third, a decision maker, whether a legislature acting with the concurrence of an executive, the leader of a division of a corporation, or someone else in a position of authority, makes an authoritative decision to choose one alternative from the considered possibilities. And finally, the decision is implemented, and a new policy takes the place of an old one.

Policy making everywhere consists of these four basic elements, and whether those steps are carried out formally or less so, organization- and context-specific differences will shape the ways that problems are identified and acted upon in each situation. Just as there are inherent differences in public policy making when contrasted with private policy making, there are other differences from organization to organization that will dictate how problems are identified and analyzed, and these procedures and circumstances can change from situation to situation. The point here is that each of these four steps has the potential to affect the process of defining the problem either directly or indirectly, and it is important that the analyst keep these "local" considerations in mind in approaching the task of problem definition.

The procedures and mechanisms through which problems are identified vary from organization to organization. As John W. Kingdon points out in his excellent book *Agendas, Alternatives, and Public Policies* (1994), the perception of problems can come from any number of indicators. These indicators can include routine statistical indicators, newspaper articles, crises and "focusing events," executive hunches, and other random and nonrandom sources. For an analyst, however, the organization's routinized problem indicators can be a mixed blessing. On one hand, they can be advantageous because they usually tend to highlight potential problems that are of a high priority to the organization. At the same time, however, these organizational routines can sometimes mask more serious problems, or they can shape the perception of problems in a way that will cause the analyst and the organization to interpret a situation incorrectly. An everyday example of this kind of misinterpretation is the reliance of some investors on the reports issued by stock analysts, when in fact it may be that those analysts have a vested interest in seeing a stock perform well. Sometimes, as a policy analyst you must set aside the usual indicators and look at the raw data yourself.

Similarly, the ways that organizations and government agencies specify the potential alternatives to their identified problems also have an impact on the process of problem definition. For the policy analyst, knowing which members of the organization should be involved in considering and deliberating on a problem will directly affect problem definition. To put this idea into perspective, consider the problem deliberation and alternative specification that we might find in examining those processes in a for-profit health care system. While any member of the organization might identify a problem with safety, staffing, the allocation of resources, profitability, health care delivery, the physical plant, or some other aspect of the system's operation, no one set of actors within the system could specify a solution to the perceived problem alone. Administrators, budget analysts (or the chief financial officer), health care professionals, and other staff members would all have to be involved in judging the potential feasibility of solutions that might be considered for system-wide adoption.

Likewise, any potential courses of action considered would necessarily involve trade-offs among the various concerns and interests represented by each segment of the system. In order to be successful in this scenario, then, the processes of problem identification and alternative specification must be carried out in a manner best described as democratic and inclusive. If you talk with health care professionals, you will find that the most successful organizations are those that have adopted this inclusive, more democratic climate of problem identification and alternative specification given the nature of the overarching organizational goals and the demands of the tasks at hand. On the contrary, if you were to examine these same processes at a civil engineering firm, you would likely find a completely different and far less inclusive style of problem identification and alternative specification at work, given the different goals and demands characteristic of that type of organization.

Similarly, the varying styles of decision making and the organization's distribution of decision-making authority will have an impact on the ways that the analyst structures the problem for analysis. Simply put, the analyst will likely tailor the definition of the problem in accordance with the stated and implied priorities of the set of organizational actors in a position to influence the final outcome in the policy area in question. In the practical world, this means that the analyst is well advised to contact all the decision makers and other influential actors at the outset of the analysis and throughout the various stages of that analysis to ensure that the effort is consistent with the goals of the organization. Likewise, the analyst is influenced by his perception of the ability of the organization to implement the policy changes that he will consider. Therefore, this consideration itself carries with it a corresponding if indirect influence over the manner in which he will define the problem at the beginning of the analytic effort.

In sum, the nature of the policy-making process within an organization will have direct and indirect effects on the ways that problems are identified and defined within the organization, and the policy analyst must be sensitive to these processes. The various steps of the policy-making process will combine to exert a subtle (and sometimes not so subtle) influence over the deliberations that take place in defining the problem. These factors shape the range of feasible policy changes that are possible in a given situation as well as the alternatives that will ultimately be considered by the organization. Accordingly, the effective policy analyst understands and takes into consideration these organization-specific features of the policy-making process in defining his or her particular problem.

2.7 Notes and Supplementary Readings

• David Dery's book on problem definition, *Problem Definition in Policy Analysis* (1984), provides another perspective on this critical step in the process of policy analysis. Dery addresses the challenges posed by alternative potential definitions, political demands, complexity, and other important factors that shape our efforts to define our policy problems. He also differentiates between institutional and organizational obstacles to problem redefinition, and he offers sample problem definitions.

• Duncan MacRae Jr. delineates the various systems of policy indicators used in public administration to assist in the identification and definition of policy problems in *Policy Indicators: Links Between Social Science and Public Debate* (1985). He examines the role of values in these systems, and he describes four general types of assessment that rely on public statistics.

• James P. Lester and Joseph Stewart Jr. differentiate between "policy analysis" and "policy research" in chapter 3 of *Public Policy: An Evolutionary Approach* (1996). They also describe alternative approaches to the task of policy analysis.

• Lewis G. Irwin describes in detail the various legislative actors and potential obstacles that are likely to stand in the way of those seeking to affect policy changes in *A Chill in the House* (2002). This account includes six legislative histories and a component-by-component analysis of changes in the policy-making process over the last several decades, as well as an assessment of the influence of legislative actors inside and outside of government.

• John W. Kingdon identifies the important ways that public problems make their way onto the public agenda in chapter 5 of *Agendas, Alternatives, and Public Policies* (1994). He addresses the primary roles of indicators, focusing events, crises, symbols, and feedback in the process of public problem identification. He also describes in detail the way that potential policy alternatives come to be considered viable as they make their way onto the "short list of ideas," a topic addressed directly in subsequent chapters of this book.

• Jean Reith Schroedel offers an additional perspective on the challenges of the legislative process, including three case histories, in chapter 3 of *Congress, the President, and Policymaking* (1994).

• Thomas A. Schwandt's *Qualitative Inquiry: A Dictionary of Terms* (1997) lists and defines a wide variety of terms and phrases that pertain to the various aspects of social inquiry.

• In *Micromotives and Macrobehavior* (1978), Thomas C. Schelling discusses the importance of "motive analysis" in predicting the potential advantages and disadvantages of public policy alternatives.

• In Paul Streeter's edited volume, *Values in Social Theory: A Selection of Essays on Methodology by Gunnar Myrdal* (1958), the editor's introduction deals at length with the normative aspects of public policy questions and the relationships between "policy" and "analysis" and the limitations of models. Similarly, the first Myrdal essay assesses the role of "values" in scientific, political, and economic inquiry.

• In chapter 6 of *Contemporary Public Policy Analysis* (1984), Stuart S. Nagel addresses the various ethical dilemmas that policy analysts face in structuring policy problems. Some of these dilemmas include the analysts' choices of which values to maximize in their analyses, the possibilities of unforeseen consequences that might result from their structuring of the problem, and the need to deal with partisan political interests and other external influences within the process.

• In *Theoretical Issues in Policy Analysis* (1988), M.E. Hawkesworth offers several examples of how influential the analyst's problem definition becomes in shaping the resultant list of potential solutions. In chapter 5, the author addresses affirmative action policies, while chapters 6, 7, and 8 deal with the issue areas of conflict resolution, human rights, and "workfare," respectively.

• In chapter 2 of Frank P. Scioli Jr. and Thomas J. Cook's *Methodologies for Analyzing Public Policies* (1975), Elinor Ostrom describes the difficulties inherent in measuring agency output and performance. She goes on to prescribe multiple output measures as a potential solution to these challenges. She also describes the differences in the assessment of public and private organizations and the additional problems that the evaluation of government agencies entails. In chapter 3 of the same edited volume, David A. Caputo remarks upon implications of the all-too-common situation in which the "customers" of public agencies, or the average citizens who receive the benefits of those agencies, are excluded from the routine assessments of agency performance. Eugene J. Meehan comments in chapter 4 on the difficulty in defining "social indicators" that will measure the health of a society's social policies.

• Chapter 2 of Duncan MacRae Jr. and James A. Wilde's *Policy Analysis for Public Decisions* (1985) outlines the challenges of problem definition, and these authors differentiate between "specific," "intermediate," and "general" problems. The authors also describe the origins of "problem situations" and ways that statistical indicators can be used to identify those situations. They use comparisons of U.S. and Soviet military expenditures and homicide rates by race as examples of this type of statistical indicator and the various interpretations that can result from their use.

• Edward A. Suchman's *Evaluative Research: Principles and Practice in Public Service and Social Action Programs* (1967) takes an in-depth look at the dynamics of public agency performance and the means through which those agencies accomplish self-evaluation. Suchman asserts that agency assessments are motivated by one of three situations: changes in the underlying social conditions that brought about the agency in the first place, changes in the agency's delivery of services, or demands for change among the segment of the public serviced by the agency. In chapter 4 of the book, Suchman differentiates among five types of evaluation, including evaluation of effort, performance, adequacy of performance, efficiency, and process.

• In the fourth and fifth sections of Edward R. Tufte's edited volume, *The Quantitative Analysis of Social Problems* (1970), a variety of authors offer their perspectives on problem definition, the use of survey data, data analysis, and research design. Of particular note, John W. Tukey and M.B. Wilk address a variety of fundamental design concerns in statistical analysis, while Leslie Kish highlights the potential pitfalls that confront the quantitative researcher.

• In chapters 1 and 2 of Arnold J. Love's edited volume, *Developing Effective Internal Evaluation* (1983), the authors describe the goals of the internal programmatic review process and the roles of internal evaluators. In chapter 1, Love identifies the organizational factors that influence the development of internal evaluation systems. In chapter 2, David L. Clifford and Paul Sherman describe the roles and skills of internal evaluators.

- *Research for Public Policy* (1961) describes a series of lectures on the uses of economic methods in assessing different types of public policies. In the first lecture, Pendleton Herring offers perspectives on research in government and public administration. In the second, Philip E. Mosely addresses policy analysis and research in the field of foreign policy, while Charles E. Hitch expands upon the general utility of economics in policy analysis in the third lecture.

- In chapter 7 of Stella A. Theodoulou and Matthew A. Cain's *Public Policy: The Essential Readings* (1995), Hugh Heclo differentiates between the once-dominant theory of the "iron triangle" and his updated model of the "issue network." Heclo also introduces the concept of the "technopol," or the political actor who specializes in one particular area of public policy, often becoming a dominant player within that particular field.

- Thomas R. Dye provides an overview of various theories of public policy making in chapter 2 of *Understanding Public Policy* (2002). Dye covers institutionalism, the process model, rationalism, incrementalism, group theory, elite theory, public choice theory, and game theory.

- In *Comparative Public Administration and Policy* (2002), Jamil E. Jreisat explains comparative research and methods in chapter 3 and then applies those techniques to the task of public policy analysis in chapter 4. Jreisat offers distinctions between the policy-making environments in developing and developed countries in chapters 5 and 6 of the book.

- George M. Guess and Paul G. Farnham explain the application of cost-effectiveness analysis as an alternative to cost-benefit analysis in chapter 6 of *Cases in Public Policy Analysis* (2000). They use a study of the transmission of HIV between mother and infant as their example of this kind of policy analysis.

- George J. Gordon elaborates on contemporary challenges that the modern policy analyst confronts in chapter 16 of his book,

Public Administration in America (1992). Among other challenges, Gordon cites the increasing social and economic diversity that analysts must contend with in their daily activities, as well as a number of tensions and paradoxes that he sees in modern public administration. Among the paradoxes that he identifies are a "revolution of rising expectations," a reliance on industrialism even in the face of "postindustrialism," and other such challenges. Gordon also argues that this heightened level of uncertainty is further exacerbated by an accelerating rate of change in administrative theory and practice.

• David Osborne and Ted Gaebler provide an alternative means of defining problems in public organizations in *Reinventing Government: How the Entrepreneurial Spirit is Transforming the Public Sector* (1992). The authors view agency performance in terms of an agency's linkage to its community and "customers," its level of competition in delivering services, its mission focus, and the results it produces over time.

3

Generating Potential Courses of Action

3.1 Where Do We Find Solutions?

In many respects, the second step of the analytical framework merely represents the logical extension of the first. That is, having decided the direction that the analysis will go in light of our preliminary examination of the problem and relevant evidence, we can next turn our attention to extending that examination of the evidence to see what potential solutions to the problem are suggested. If we have defined our policy problem effectively, then we will already have some notions about the features that we will need to incorporate into any workable solution to our problem. Furthermore, at this point we will already have developed ideas about the root causes of our problem, and, although not wholly confident of these notions yet, we will use these desired features and ideas about plausible causes of the problem as the basis for our generation of potential solutions.

Armed with our problem definition then, we begin to generate ideas about potential solutions to our problem. As we start this process, we take a "blue sky" approach, meaning that we are unlimited in our thinking and we are now willing to consider a wide variety of potential courses of action (COAs). At this point, we will seek ideas from a wide variety of sources, and we merely add the ideas to our working list of COAs without regard for their feasibility or desirability. Put another way, it is important that we avoid assessing the potential COAs at this point. Now is the time for creativity and imagination, rather than critical analysis.

It is important that we consult with others and look outside our own experience for potential solutions to our problem at this point in the policy analysis. There are a number of ways that we can achieve this broader perspective, and the first activity that we usually engage in when confronted by this task is "brainstorming." Brainstorming can be an individual activity, but it is most effective when it is done as a group exercise. We brainstorm by working at the problem at hand through a relatively unstructured group discussion of the problem, its root causes, and potential COAs that could address the problem. It is always most effective to include both subject-matter experts and nonspecialists in the group in order to avoid the tendency to stray too far from reality while still considering new ideas and revisiting time-honored assumptions. It is often quite helpful to be forced to articulate aloud the logic and rationale behind the policy changes that we are beginning to consider.

In addition, we have other avenues to pursue in our search for potential COAs that might help us solve our policy problem. We conduct additional research at this point, including primary and secondary source document analyses, and we interview other people to ask how they have dealt with similar problems in the past. Frequently in policy circles you will hear this idea of consultation with others in similar circumstances referred to as "best practices" research, or the search for the "best" solution employed by others in order to apply that solution to your own situation. Given the challenges of particularity described in chapter 1, however, and although "best practice" is an effective way to generate additional ideas for our working list of potential COAs, we should always proceed cautiously before assuming that solutions that worked elsewhere will work in our own invariably unique conditions. Nevertheless, we talk to others inside and outside of our organization and we search for written accounts of successful approaches to similar problems as an effective way to enhance our own generation of potential solutions.

Finally, the decision maker is a good source of ideas about potential changes that we might consider in constructing our working list of potential problem solutions. In any event, we will consult with the decision maker at this stage of the analysis to get his or her ideas about potential COAs for practical reasons as well as analytical ones. In fact, while I have listed the decision maker last in this list of potential sources of ideas about problem solutions, frequently the decision maker's proposed policy change was the driving force behind the analysis in the first place. If this is so, then we will certainly add this COA to our list. However, the point here of listing the decision maker last is to call attention to the fact that his ideas are among many that we will want to consider as we pursue the goal of objective rationality. Part of our "value-added" as policy analysts is taking a broader perspective on the consideration of the problem at hand.

Once we have done our brainstorming and consulting, we then have our unconstrained working list of potential COAs. Most often, this working list is a rather general list of ideas that will need to be refined further before we can analyze them with any rigor. Moreover, it is usual to have to revisit the first step of the process, our problem definition, at this point in the policy analysis. In light of the new ideas and new evidence that we will have collected during the generation of our working list of potential COAs, we may need to revise or refine our definition of the problem prior to moving forward in the analysis. As noted before, policy analysis is an iterative process, and we may work in fits and starts, particularly in the first few steps of the process. Nevertheless, once we have generated a working list of potential COAs, we are ready to take our next step forward in the policy analysis.

3.2   The Status Quo

As part of our working list of potential alternatives, we always include the status quo, or the choice of maintaining the existing policy in place, as an option. We do this for several reasons. First, the status quo serves as the baseline against which we will evaluate the other potential COAs that make it onto our eventual short list of options, performing an important function in our analysis that becomes apparent as we get further into the comparison of alternatives. Second, the status quo represents a real option, since the decision to maintain a policy in place involves the allocation of resources and expenditure of those resources with resulting consequences. Along these same lines, it is important for the analyst and decision maker to realize that although the status quo policy has produced certain results under past conditions, the future will not necessarily hold the same prospects. It is important for us to take a close look at the consequences of the current policy as we project it into the conditions likely to arise in the future. Finally, as it often turns out that the status quo represents the best potential COA for the future when all of the analysis is done, we always want to consider the status quo on our working list. It is always an option to stay the course, even in the face of political pressure to the contrary.

3.3 Selecting the Short List

With our working list of potential COAs in hand, we turn our attention to a preliminary evaluation of the COAs and the generation of our short list of alternatives. In this step in the generation of COAs, our goal is to reduce our "blue sky" list of wide-ranging policy options to a compact list of a few feasible and potentially desirable policy alternatives that will merit careful and intense scrutiny. While we have been careful to this point not to evaluate alternatives, aiming instead to construct an unconstrained list of ideas to consider, we begin now to trim our list as we start assessing the merits of the potential policy changes. This step in the process will likely involve additional research as we seek to refine our understanding of the likely prospects that correspond to the potential policy changes that we will consider. However, we will also find that by now this additional research is becoming increasingly focused on specific topics.

Before we begin this procedure, however, it is helpful to revisit our problem definition one more time. The goal here is to remind ourselves of the essence of the problem that we are attempting to address, so that we can ensure that we focus upon alternatives that do in fact have positive consequences for the situation to which we are responding. With this idea in mind, our first sweep through the list is aimed at identifying and eliminating any options that, on second thought, do not actually address our problem. It is not uncommon for us to include in our working list solutions used by others in somewhat similar circumstances, only to realize as we consider our list that some aspect of our case prevents that solution from working in our circumstances. This is a healthy and normal occurrence, and it is better to eliminate those potential solutions at the outset of consideration than to invest time (and subsequent credibility) in analyzing them further, only to realize their impracticality later in the process. So our first task is to eliminate potential COAs that will have little or no positive impact on the underlying problem we seek to solve. We must cross those potential COAs off our list.

Similarly, our second sweep through the working list is aimed at identifying and eliminating those potential COAs that are not feasible. In this sweep, we identify the potential COAs that would likely have a positive impact on our basic problem but would be either difficult or impossible to implement in any meaningful and realistic way. These difficulties could include, for example, the likelihood of funding, unrealistic assumptions, issues of legality or constitutionality, or other aspects of the COA itself that would make it unlikely that the policy change could ever be implemented.

For our third sweep, we would examine our working list for potential COAs that might be likely to fail owing to political considerations and other contextual constraints. These political considerations could be literal blocs of opposition within the bodies holding important decision-making authority or more common organizational predispositions and concerns. Some potentially plausible policy changes just do not work within some organizations or for some decision makers, and it is a waste of time to consider them in your analysis unless there are previously unconsidered aspects of the COA that might outweigh some of those usual concerns. In any event, during this third sweep we take a hard look at our list to identify potential COAs that will be likely to elicit serious contextual or political opposition down the line.

If all is right in your analytical world, at this point you will have developed a short list of between two and five potential COAs, including the status quo, that you will consider for your eventual policy recommendation. The consideration of more than four new policy alternatives within the context of one analytical project is usually unwieldy. Therefore, if you find at this point that you have more than four COAs in addition to the status quo, it is usually a good idea to reduce your list further. In this final sweep, you will apply the criteria of the first three sweeps again and your own judgment to prioritize your potential COAs and reduce your short list to a manageable size.

If, on the other hand, you have performed the first three sweeps only to have eliminated all of your "blue sky" options from the working list, you have a different kind of choice to face. You can start generating ideas again, expanding your research and consulting to generate a larger working list, then applying the criteria of the first three sweeps again to determine whether there are in fact positive, feasible, and practical options to consider. Or, alternatively, you can conclude that there are no such options to consider for the time being, an analytical finding in itself. You would then take this analysis and your finding to the decision maker, after which you both can decide how best to continue from there. Your individual circumstances and judgment will drive that choice.

However, for most analysts this process will result in a short list of potential COAs that you will begin to consider in much more detail as the next step in the analytical process. It should be noted here that the fact that you are considering the merits of these alternatives compared to one another and the status quo does not imply that they are necessarily mutually exclusive options. In fact, it is often the case that our eventual policy recommendations take the form of a package of several recommended policy changes. These changes can be independent of one another or they can be mutually supporting. At this stage of our policy analysis, however, we have once again defined our problem more precisely, and we prepare to begin our detailed analysis and subsequent comparison of the COAs.

3.4 Defining the Alternatives Up Front

Once we have generated our short list of potential COAs, the next step in our problem formulation is to define them more precisely. This is a critical step, because it is at this point that we truly begin to chart our potential policy recommendations. Taking the time to define our COAs carefully at this point again focuses our analysis and our data collection efforts and saves us time later in the analysis. The precise definition of our potential policy options also enables us to identify the advantages and disadvantages of each COA more easily and enhances the validity of our results.

By way of illustration, consider the implications of precision of COA definition for an analysis of educational system reforms. After working through the generation of potential COAs, we have included on our short list "tuition vouchers" as feasible, desirable, and practical. While most policy analysts active in this field would understand the concept in question, there are any number of variations of these vouchers. Examples of the potential differences include variable eligibility requirements, different payment methods, variations in the dollar value of the voucher alternatives, and so forth. So although the phrase "tuition vouchers" captures an important idea with relevance to the underlying problem that we are trying to address, it is also true that different kinds of voucher plans are going to have considerably different implications for the education system viewed as a whole.

That is, we will need to define a number of important aspects of the potential policy changes carefully in order to make accurate predictions about the likely effects of those changes. A voucher plan that allows parents of school-aged children to forgo property tax payments to pay parochial school tuition will have much different consequences from those of a plan that precludes the usage of the tax credit in parochial schools. This consideration is one of many that will have serious implications for the outcome of any policy change.

Furthermore, the process of carefully defining the potential COAs may also force us to consider variants of the same basic course of action. Using the tuition voucher example, we may end up needing to analyze two or more variations of the basic voucher idea, including a "$1,500 option," a "$3,000 option," and so forth. Alternatively, we might decide to make assumptions about these characteristics in light of some estimate of the probabilities of particular outcomes or our own judgments of feasibility or practicality. In any event, we make these choices up front and then justify the choices that we make. Finally, as we continue to compile the specific information needed to define the potential COAs more carefully, we will also continue to extend our understanding of the basic problem we are trying to solve and the aspects of the problem that are most important to us. Now we are ready to begin our analysis of the COAs.

3.5 Transitioning to the Analysis of the Alternatives

Once we have completed our careful definition of the potential COAs, we have also completed our creation of the short list that we will analyze using one or the other of the major analytical techniques. We are ready to transition to the analysis and comparison of the courses of action as we move toward our policy recommendation. During the process of defining our problem and generating our potential COAs, we will have begun to identify the criteria that are most important to us, considerations that have to be fulfilled by any solution that we might recommend. After giving some thought to these concerns, we settle upon the criterion or set of criteria that we will use to evaluate the alternatives.

Once we have completed this selection of criteria, our next step in the process is the application of either cost-benefit analysis (CBA) or multi-attribute analysis (MAA) in analyzing the merits of the COAs on our short list. (These techniques and the criteria that correspond to them are examined in more detail in chapters 4 and 5.) The choice of analytical method is fairly straightforward. When an analyst or decision maker has as his primary concern the consideration of efficiency or a desire to allocate scarce resources in a way that provides the best net benefit for society or for a particular constituency within it, CBA is the technique of choice. Conversely, when the analyst or decision maker has a variety of concerns, whether utilitarian or normative, and seeks to satisfy all of them as best she can with the optimal mix of variables, then MAA is the logical choice.

3.6 Notes and Supplementary Readings

• Garry D. Brewer and Peter deLeon examine the challenges and importance of alternative generation in detail in chapter 3 of *The Foundations of Policy Analysis* (1983). They contend that the generation of policy alternatives has long been the primary task expected of the policy analyst, and they seek to place this step of the process into its proper context as an important but intermingled part of a larger process.

• David Nachmias addresses the difficulties inherent in the search for policy solutions in chapter 1 of his edited volume, *The Practice of Policy Evaluation* (1980). In chapter 9 of the book, Aaron Wildavsky expands upon that subject, turning his attention to the common shortcomings of organizational policy assessment and self-evaluation.

• Hugh Heclo describes the "issue network," or collection of experts, administrators, politicians, and other players who tend to dominate the identification of potential policy solutions, in Anthony King's edited volume, *The New American Political System* (1978).

• John W. Kingdon envisions the "policy primeval soup" that gives rise to a resultant "short list of ideas" in *Agendas, Alternatives, and Public Policies* (1994). This "short list of ideas" is the working list of possible problem solutions that emerges in the consideration of public policy problems.

• As noted in chapters 2 and 3, the policy-making process itself will constrain the range of feasible policy changes available to the analyst for realistic consideration. Michael Hill places the activities of policy projection, policy assessment, and information gathering within the context of the broader policy-making process in *The Policy Process in the Modern State* (1997). In chapter 1 of his book, Hill also addresses the origins of the ongoing debates over the merits and shortcomings of quantitative techniques of policy assessment and the solutions that these techniques suggest. He further describes the various products that can result from the analytic process, among them studies of the policy process, studies of policy outputs, evaluation studies, and policy change advocacy. Frank P. Scioli Jr. and Thomas J. Cook offer their own description of these various analytical objectives in chapter 1 of their edited volume, *Methodologies for Analyzing Public Policies* (1975). In chapter 7 of that book, E. Terrence Jones comments on the differences between analyzing incremental policy adjustments and major policy changes. These considerations are important given that incremental policy changes occur far more frequently than radical policy overhauls.

• In chapter 4 of *Theoretical Issues in Policy Analysis* (1988), M.E. Hawkesworth cautions against the fabrication of false alternatives based upon faulty problem construction.

• Chapter 3 of Duncan MacRae Jr. and James A. Wilde's *Policy Analysis for Public Decisions* (1985) offers an alternative perspective on the selection and application of evaluative criteria. The authors identify the implications of choosing what they call ethical criteria such as "freedom" and "equality," and they also address criteria such as "desirability" and "political feasibility" before turning their attention to cost-benefit analyses and "equity."

• In chapter 21 of Stella A. Theodoulou and Matthew A. Cain's *Public Policy: The Essential Readings* (1995), Irene S. Rubin describes the particular challenges presented by the politics of public budgeting. She outlines the roles and functions of the budget in public agencies, and she comments on the ways that budgetary factors often constrain the range of feasible policy changes that an analyst may consider from the outset of the analytic process.

• George M. Guess and Paul G. Farnham provide an alternative explanation of the technique of cost-benefit analysis in chapter 7 of *Cases in Public Policy Analysis* (2000). The authors also provide an example of the generation of policy alternatives and the type of analysis that results from those alternatives. In chapter 7, the authors provide an analysis of proposed changes in environmental policies intended to improve air quality standards.

• In chapter 2 of *The Policy Puzzle* (1996), Donald T. Wells and Chris R. Hamilton offer an outline of the evolution of American government and its responses to societal needs and demands for policy change over the twentieth century. James P. Lester and Joseph Stewart Jr. offer their own perspectives on the same subject in *Public Policy: An Evolutionary Approach* (1996).

• Part III of Eugene Bardach's *A Practical Guide to Policy Analysis* (2000) provides an overview of "best practices" or "smart practices" approaches to the generation of potential courses of action.

• David L. Weimer and Aidan R. Vining offer an alternative perspective on the generation of potential solutions to policy problems in chapter 11 of *Policy Analysis: Concepts and Practice* (1999).

4

Cost-Benefit Analysis

4.1 The Sole Criterion

We apply the technique of *cost-benefit analysis* (CBA) in our policy analysis when we are most concerned with the criterion of efficiency. In the context of policy analysis, the term "efficiency" refers to the allocation of scarce resources in a way that maximizes the resulting net benefits of that resource allocation. Put another way, efficiency, as it relates to CBA, refers to achieving our best possible "return on investment" for our money. In a sense, efficiency is very closely related to the idea of utility, except that whereas utility usually refers to the greatest amount of good for the greatest number of people, efficiency seeks to maximize the benefits available to a target group or constituency. In policy analysis, this target group or constituency can be (and often is) society in general, but it is just as often a client, organization, city, or some other segment of the population. In any event, we adopt the CBA technique and the sole criterion of efficiency when our goal is to determine the policy that provides the largest net benefit possible to the target group relative to the cost of the policy change. CBA uses money as the primary unit of analysis in achieving this analytical goal, as we translate the likely effects of the proposed policy changes into a summary of associated costs and benefits.

Obviously, however, not all of the consequences of most policy changes can be reduced to dollar terms, and therefore the use of this sole evaluative criterion is a simplifying and limiting assumption.

While this simplifying assumption does not entirely preclude the inclusion of normative and "intangible" concerns in the CBA, it is often difficult, if not impossible, to capture these normative considerations in any meaningful way once the CBA is underway. For example, consider a fairly typical subject of CBA, the decision of whether to build a dam in a local community. In order to build the dam, the government will likely have to exercise the right of eminent domain, or the right of the government to appropriate private property in order to convert that property to public use, because once the dam fills, it will flood some of the surrounding land. Often when dams are built, people are forced to abandon their homes, receiving compensation for this forced relocation in return. This exercise of eminent domain, from the government decision makers' perspectives, comes with a tangible cost in the form of the dollar cost of the compensation paid to the landowners.

However, while this compensation addresses one aspect of the exercise of eminent domain, at the same time there are issues of fairness, inconvenience, environmental risk, and other considerations that are far less tangible, though quite real, representing different kinds of "costs" of the project. Viewing the issue of the construction of the dam in these terms, how can we put practical dollar values on the "costs" of "sentimental value," "fairness," or "inconvenience," for example? Any logic that we apply in trying to capture those normative and intangible costs is likely to be tenuous at best. Therefore, it is important for us as policy analysts to realize that the application of CBA certainly works well in satisfying the criterion of efficiency, but it simplifies the problem as well. As a result, CBA frequently ignores some of the most consequential implications of potential policy changes from the perspective of those who will personally feel the effects of the change. We must consider these implications before we settle on the CBA as our analytical technique with its sole criterion of efficiency.

Nevertheless, CBA is the most common formal analytical technique that you will come across in policy circles, and it is very effective when applied correctly and appropriately. Furthermore, while CBA does not lend itself readily to the incorporation of normative and less tangible considerations in our policy analyses, there are ways to work around this inherent challenge of the technique while preserving the rationality that the method offers. The first way that we can do this is to deal with the normative concerns and "intangibles" in our problem definition and the generation of our short list of potential courses of action (COAs). For example, if we are building a dam, we might decide to consider only options that would limit the exercise of eminent domain, an approach that might be desirable for political reasons as well as reasons of associated costs. Additionally, we might preclude from consideration all options that are likely to damage the surrounding environment.

As an alternative method, we might also go ahead with our CBA to determine the net benefits or costs of the competing COAs, but then also add an additional section in our analysis. In this section, we would briefly identify and compare the "uncaptured" normative or intangible concerns that would also be likely to result from the adoption of the respective COAs. In this way, we would identify these important concerns to the decision maker, paving the way for him to take those concerns into consideration prior to making any final decision. This approach is particularly appropriate in the cases in which the competing COAs are very similar in terms of the net benefits that they offer or the efficiency that they realize. In these cases, the normative or intangible considerations might serve as "tie-breakers," whereas in other cases the decision makers might be inclined to choose an option that offers a better mix of these intangibles even if that mix comes at a minor cost of efficiency. In any event, the associated costs and benefits of a potential policy change are frequently the most important considerations for a decision maker, and as a result the CBA technique is often the appropriate analytical technique to use. However, it is still important that we make an "eyes open" choice when selecting our analytical technique and corresponding criteria, so that we do not overlook other important aspects of the potential policy changes that we are analyzing.

4.2   Identifying the Advantages and Disadvantages

Armed with our short list of clearly defined potential COAs, we next turn our attention to their various advantages and disadvantages. Although we have selected our evaluative criterion at this point in the analytic process, we approach the generation of this list of advantages and disadvantages unconstrained by that criterion. This means that we list every potential advantage and disadvantage we can imagine, regardless of whether we believe the particular effect of that characteristic likely to be positive, negative, tangible, intangible, or normative in nature. Our goal at this point is to think through the potential COAs thoroughly in order to identify every consequence of the COA. When we are applying the cost-benefit technique of analysis, we expect that many of these advantages and disadvantages are going to correspond to costs or benefits that we will identify later, but many will not. The goal here is to identify all of the potential upsides and downsides of the COAs, irrespective of cost or benefit for the moment.

Once we have identified all of the advantages and disadvantages of the various COAs, including the status quo, we take a moment to review our results to this point. Are we still confident that we have selected the right criterion and analytical technique in light of the various advantages and disadvantages? Have we identified all of the advantages and disadvantages that we can, or are there other advantages and disadvantages suggested by one COA that might correspond to other COAs? Like the other steps in the analytical process, this one is iterative. Therefore, it is all right if we decide at this point to refine our lists of advantages and disadvantages, to change our evaluative criteria, or even to revisit our basic problem definitions and major assumptions. Additionally, it is healthy to review the empirical evidence that we gathered in carefully defining our COAs in order to make sure that we have not missed anything of importance in putting together these important lists of potential good points and bad points.

4.3   Data Collection and Assumptions

Once we have generated these important lists of advantages and disadvantages for each of our potential COAs, we begin the process of translating these advantages and disadvantages into the costs and benefits that we will use to generate our policy recommendations. Essentially, this step in the process involves culling the lists of advantages and disadvantages to identify all of the potential effects that will correspond to some costs or benefits and then gathering the data needed to enable us to predict what those associated costs and benefits might be. While this step might sound fairly easy, it is in fact a very challenging phase in our analysis and is often hard to do well.

As noted in chapter 1, prediction is usually the most difficult goal to achieve for any social scientist, and this goal is particularly tricky for the policy analyst. Yet the ability to predict the consequences of a prospective policy change is the essence of the analytical task, and therefore we devote much energy to trying to get it right. In order to increase our chances of successful prediction, wherever possible we base our predictions upon empirical evidence and analysis rather than on mere assumptions or logic alone. This means searching for cases in which similar COAs were adopted under comparable circumstances and identifying the subsequent effects of the implementation of that COA, and then basing our own predictions on those data whenever we can. Depending upon the nature of the policy problem, however, this may be more or less practical, for reasons of availability of data and time to the analyst. But it is always desirable for us to base our predictions upon empirical data whenever possible, as our results are always stronger and more convincing when grounded in observation.

In order to predict the costs and benefits associated with a potential COA, we will have to identify particular kinds of evidence that relate directly to each of the potential advantages and disadvantages that are likely to come with some tangible cost or benefit. This task can be easier for some policy problems than for others, and the challenge of predicting costs and benefits can differ even within the same policy problem. For example, consider the case of a fire company that is considering whether to purchase a new truck that comes with equipment that the company does not have. While it is a relatively simple matter to gather the actual cost data associated with the purchase of the truck itself, it is a bit more difficult to predict the benefit of the new equipment in terms of property saved. To estimate the benefits that might accrue to the community as a result of having the new equipment available, we could look at comparably sized communities with and without the equipment. We could then examine how often the new equipment had been used in those communities, and we could compare the number of times the equipment had been used and the amount of property damage that occurred in communities with or without that type of equipment. We could then generate an estimate of the property savings in dollars that we might be likely to realize given the availability of this new equipment. To strengthen our predictions in this step in our data collection, we search for useful data such as these that correspond to all of our potential costs and benefits.

Nevertheless, even when we find these useful data, the challenge of particularity means that we will always have to incorporate some assumptions into our analysis, since we are unlikely to find comparable cases that are exactly like our own circumstances. In the best case, these merely involve tailoring our gathered empirical evidence to the particular circumstances of our own problem, as we pause to speculate upon the potential differences in outcome that might result from the different circumstances that we face. In other cases, these might be wholesale assumptions that necessarily assume away key aspects of the larger policy problem. But in any event, the key task at this point in the analysis is to identify all of our major assumptions and to scrutinize them to make sure that they make sense according to both the evidence available to us and our own reasoning. Later in the analytical process, with our findings in hand, we will revisit and challenge those assumptions to test the validity and sensitivity of our results. But for now our objective is to identify and inspect those assumptions to assess whether they are reasonable and appropriate in light of everything we have learned through our data collection and our consideration of the problem.

4.4   Predicting Costs and Benefits

Having gathered the data necessary to estimate the likely costs and benefits associated with the various potential COAs, we then make our predictions of those costs and benefits. For example, suppose we are interested in estimating one of the potential costs associated with a COA that involves the implementation of a tuition voucher program. We have defined the option carefully with a basic tuition credit of up to $5,000 available to each eligible student per school year. If we are interested in estimating the magnitude of the cost to be absorbed by the public schools that will lose tax receipts compared to the status quo policy, we have to incorporate a number of factors in our prediction. While we have carefully defined our potential COA, including the specific eligibility criteria as well as the means through which the COA would be implemented, we will still need to have collected other data or made assumptions in order to estimate this cost. Among these data and assumptions are estimates of how many students will use the program, whether they will use the full benefit or only a part of the $5,000 possible, whether there are state matching funds that will be lost in this case, and other such considerations. As you can see, in the ideal case we would look to other school systems that had made similar changes and use their experiences as the basis for our own estimates. However, if no such cases are available for analysis, then we are faced with the task of making reasoned estimates based upon careful assumptions. Whenever possible, however, we work to find the empirical evidence that will reinforce our analysis.

After we have subjected each of the identified potential costs and benefits to this kind of scrutiny, we capture our estimated potential costs and benefits of the various COAs in a tabular format. This table will serve as a powerful visual summary of our analysis, and it also helps us to make sure that we have accounted for all of the potential costs and benefits that might correspond to each

Table 4.1

An Example of a Cost-Benefit Analysis Summary Table

Course of action	Equipment Purchase Decision, Five-year Horizon		
	Estimated potential benefits	Estimated potential costs	Net benefit/(cost)
COA 1 (Purchase equipment type A)	$75,000—net profit estimate for 5 years $5,000—net resale estimate in 5 years $3,000—resale estimate for current equipment now	$10,000—purchase cost $7,500—maintenance agreement, 5 years $15,000—operating costs for 5 years $1,000—operator training	$49,500
COA 2 (Purchase equipment type B)	$95,000—net profit estimate for 5 years $10,000—net resale estimate in 5 years $3,000—resale estimate for current equipment now	$20,000—purchase cost $12,500—maintenance agreement, 5 years $20,000—operating costs for 5 years $1,000—operator training	$54,500
COA 3 (Status quo/use currently owned equipment)	$40,000—net profit estimate for 5 years $1,000—net resale estimate for current equipment in 5 years	$0—purchase cost $18,000—maintenance agreement, 5 years $25,000—operating costs for 5 years $0—operator training	($2,000)

Note: COA = course of action.

potential COA. Table 4.1 shows an example of such a table as it would be used to help make a relatively simple decision, for example, whether to purchase some new type of equipment. As this example shows, we also include in the table an overall net cost or benefit of each COA, as well as brief labels on the COAs and the potential costs and benefits. These results serve as the basis for our overall policy recommendation once we have evaluated the sensitivity of our assumptions and estimates.

In this simplified example, which neglects time-value of money considerations and encompasses only a few costs and benefits, we still find many aspects of the basic challenges of the CBA technique well represented. While the purchase costs, maintenance agreement costs, and operating costs might be rather straightforward estimates based on easily gathered data, the net profit prediction for each COA might be more difficult to estimate. This predicted value might depend on a wide variety of factors, ranging from economic forecasts to projected equipment usage schedules and other variables, both on the supply and demand sides of the equation. Furthermore, it is easy to see that this net profit estimate represents the greatest portion of the likely benefits we will receive from the proposed change, and therefore it is likely that our results will be quite sensitive to shifts in these estimates. We also see from the net benefit/cost column that while our analysis clearly indicates that a new equipment purchase is the way to go, the choice between COAs 1 and 2 represents a less significant difference. With this in mind, if we have other normative or less tangible considerations that would also matter to us, we might be inclined to "value" that difference or others at greater than the $5,000 difference in net benefit. Such a difference might include how "environmentally friendly" equipment A is compared to equipment B, different maintenance histories, or some other factors.

4.5   Net Benefits as Probabilities

In some cases, however, we are not able to identify only one likely outcome of a proposed COA as it pertains to one associated cost or benefit. In this situation, we may decide either to construct a probability tree or to calculate an expected value based on our estimate of the chances of each possible outcome. In the case of the probability tree, this approach essentially involves turning our net benefit calculations into a set of estimates, with a different net benefit corresponding to each of the likely possibilities. For example, if we look once again at Table 4.1, our estimate of operating costs might be driven by the use of a certain amount of fuel at a certain price per gallon. We might have different notions about what that price will be over our five-year horizon, and we may think it possible that two or three different price levels might be possible. In this case, we might construct a probability tree in which we estimate the probability of one scenario occurring at 50 percent, with another scenario at 25 percent, and a third also at 25 percent. In this way, we could capture the various possibilities explicitly, giving the decision maker the chance to make the decision based on these possibly contrasting scenarios.

Alternatively, we might want to capture those various probabilities in our one overall estimate of the net benefit corresponding to the potential COA. With this idea in mind, we would calculate an *expected value* for the operating cost based on the probabilities associated with the various price levels we anticipate as possibilities. That is, we would take our first price level, calculate the cost corresponding to that price level, and multiply that estimated cost by a factor of .50. We would do the same for each of the other two scenarios, multiplying both of those results by the .25 probability corresponding to those price levels. We would then sum all three figures that resulted, and we would use that *expected value* as our figure for the operating cost, even though it would probably not correspond to an actual value associated with any of the three expected price levels. In this way, however, we would have captured the probabilities inherent in the operating cost in our one overarching estimate of the probable net benefit of the COA.

4.6 Sensitivity and Assumption Analysis

At this point, we are one important step away from being prepared to conclude our CBA. We next analyze our results in terms of their sensitivity to changes in the important assumptions that we have made in the course of our policy analysis. It is generally beyond the scope of our effort to subject all of the assumptions we make to this scrutiny, so we select for checking the most important and most influential assumptions and reasoning that we have incorporated into the analysis. Basically, sensitivity analysis involves applying a "best case/ worst case" test to these assumptions in order to gauge whether our findings would change significantly if those assumptions were off the mark somewhat. In order to carry out the sensitivity analysis, we recalculate our net benefits to find "best case" and "worst case" estimated net benefits for each of the critical assumptions in turn.

If we find that our results are not very sensitive to changes in our key assumptions, then we are usually quite confident of our analysis, and we merely review everything once before making our policy recommendation. If, on the other hand, we discover that our results are in fact very sensitive to the key assumptions, we have a few options. First of all, understand that this sensitivity does not mean that we will reject our analysis, as it is not uncommon for our analyses to be sensitive to those critical assumptions. However, we do have some choices to make in light of this information. We may decide to revisit those key assumptions, gathering further data in order to reinforce our belief that the assumptions are valid. We can then present our analysis as is, noting for the decision maker what the key assumptions are as well as the fact that the results are sensitive to relatively modest changes in those key estimates.

Alternatively, we may revisit our recommendation altogether, particularly if we perceive that the uncertainty involved in the selection of one sensitive COA might make that option much riskier than some other comparable but less sensitive alternative. In other words, we might select a less attractive but less uncertain option in light of the sensitivity analysis, particularly if our confidence in our own assessment of the critical assumptions is fairly low. The bottom line here is that uncertainty in an analyst's recommendation is not a sin, particularly if it is uncertainty based upon a careful consideration of the basic problem at hand. You make the best call that you can, but you also understand the limits of the information and reasoning upon which that call is made.

As a final consideration at this point in the CBA, we also include a paragraph or so in our prose after the summary table that mentions the other normative and "intangible" costs and benefits that also bear on the problem. We do this for a few reasons. First of all, we do it to show that our analysis is thorough, and that while these factors are not included in our analysis formally, they were not ignored during the analytical process. Second, we mention these "uncaptured" advantages and disadvantages in the prose in case they can serve as "tie-breakers" when the decision maker is confronted with comparable efficiency among the potential COAs. Finally, we include these considerations in our analysis because some decision makers will decide to accept a minor loss of efficiency in exchange for a gain in those normative or intangible concerns. Chapter 6 deals with these and other considerations that surround the actual policy recommendation itself.

4.7 Notes and Supplementary Readings

• Stuart S. Nagel assesses effectiveness, efficiency, and equity as alternative policy goals in chapter 3 of *Policy Studies: Integration and Evaluation* (1988), and he discusses some strategies for achieving "multidimensionality" in our analyses in that chapter. He offers a justification for the cost-benefit technique's efficiency criterion in this chapter as well.

• In chapter 3 of Frank Fischer and John Forester's edited volume, *Confronting Values in Policy Analysis* (1987), John Byrne offers perspectives on the trade-offs between political interests, decision-making discipline, and solution comprehensiveness inherent in the cost-benefit approach to public problem solving. Byrne also addresses the advantages and disadvantages of public choices based upon the sole criterion of Pareto optimality. Byrne criticizes what he sees as the two flawed premises of the cost-benefit technique, including the desirability of "systematizing" policy analysis and a mismatch between the nonnormative solutions offered to normative questions by the technique.

• George M. Guess and Paul G. Farnham explain how to use various methods to forecast policy options in chapter 4 of *Cases in Public Policy Analysis* (2000). The authors cover causal and deductive forecasts, observational and inductive forecasts, and experiential forecasts. They also address trend extrapolation and regression analysis in the chapter. Guess and Farnham provide case examples of each of the techniques described.

• George M. Guess and Paul G. Farnham also explain the application of cost-effectiveness analysis as an alternative to cost-benefit analysis in chapter 6 of *Cases in Public Policy Analysis* (2000). They use a study of the transmission of HIV between mother and infant as their example of this kind of policy analysis. In chapter 7 of the book, the authors provide a fairly detailed example of cost-benefit analysis in their analysis of changes in environmental protection policy and air quality standards enacted in the 1990s.

• In chapter 5 of *Policy Indicators* (1985), Duncan MacRae Jr. examines the utility of "net economic benefit" calculations, or the cost-benefit technique, in practical policy models. Rosemarie Tong offers another critique of the technique from a sociological perspective in chapter 1 of *Ethics in Policy Analysis* (1986).

• Grant Cameron and Ross Ezzeddin elaborate upon the direct and indirect effects of changes in social policies in chapter 3 of Lavinia Mitton, Holly Sutherland, and Melvyn Weeks's (eds.) *Microsimulation Modelling for Policy Analysis* (2000).

• In their edited volume *Public Policy and Statistics: Case Studies from RAND* (2000), Sally C. Morton and John E. Rolph present case studies in policy analysis that illustrate the ways that various statistics can be used to support alternative assessments.

• Robert Formaini examines the underlying logic and strategic choices that correspond to the cost-benefit technique in chapter 3 of *The Myth of Scientific Public Policy* (1990). He further describes the relationship between the development of the cost-benefit technique and the subsequent emergence of sophisticated economic applications of this approach.

• B. Guy Peters places cost-benefit analysis into context as he summarizes the analytic technique in his chapter on policy analysis in *American Public Policy* (2000).

• Michael C. Munger explains time value of money calculations as they relate to cost-benefit analysis in chapters 9 and 10 of *Analyzing Policy: Choices, Conflicts, and Practices* (2000).

• In chapters 10, 11, and 12 of Frank Fischer and John Forester's edited volume, *Confronting Values in Policy Analysis* (1987), the various authors offer examples of efficiency-based policy analyses and the respective advantages and shortcomings of each study. In chapter 10, Susan A. Fainstein examines an analysis of urban redevelopment policy, while Steven Maynard-Moody and Donald D. Stull assess the analysis of changes in the Kansas Department of Health and Environment in 1983 in chapter 11. Charles Noble's chapter 12 takes a similar look at the White House's assessment and oversight of the Occupational Safety and Health Administration between 1981 and 1983.

• In chapter 8 of Frank P. Scioli Jr. and Thomas J. Cook's *Methodologies for Analyzing Public Policies* (1975), Stuart S. Nagel describes the logic underlying quantitative techniques for optimizing particular variable values in the face of scarce public resources. In chapters 10 and 11, the authors provide the details of the application of two related methods, with L.A. Wilson II describing statistical techniques in time series research designs in chapter 11 and Thomas R. Dye and Neuman F. Pollack explaining path analytic models in chapter 12. In chapter 13, Ronald W. Johnson and John M. Pierce provide an alternative perspective on cost-benefit analysis and the related technique of cost-effectiveness analysis.

• Chapter 5 of Duncan MacRae Jr. and James A. Wilde's *Policy Analysis for Public Decisions* (1985) addresses the potential shortcomings and benefits of a variety of economic models and the influence of a variety of factors on the performance of those models.

• Frederick S. Weaver provides an overview of the principles of macroeconomic analysis and the common measures of economic performance in chapter 3 of *Economic Literacy* (2002). In chapter 4, Weaver differentiates between the various types of economic policy and the contextual factors and recurring cycles that affect economic analysis.

5

Multi-Attribute Analysis

5.1 Multiple Criteria and Normative Concerns

While cost-benefit analysis (CBA) is quite effective in enabling us to identify the course of action (COA) likely to provide the most efficient solution to our policy problem, oftentimes we have serious concerns other than efficiency that are driving our search for a solution from the outset of our analysis. In these cases, we apply the technique of *multi-attribute analysis* (MAA) in order to identify the potential course of action that offers the most desirable combination of those characteristics of interest. MAA is quite similar to CBA in its application, with the key difference being that in MAA we select multiple evaluative criteria rather than the sole criterion of efficiency. In addition, this method differs from CBA in that we also must subsequently weight those criteria in light of our problem definition, the evidence, and our judgment in order to generate a solution to our policy problem that is properly balanced in its assessment of those other key concerns. In sum, MAA expands our consideration of our policy problem by affording us the opportunity to include a wide variety of concerns into a formal and rational problem-solving framework similar to that of CBA.

For example, think about the problem of homelessness that we considered in an earlier chapter. Certainly in this policy area, like most others, efficiency is always a serious concern. That is, any COA that a city might adopt regarding the problem of homelessness would likely come at some dollar cost of implementation, and the political leaders and administrators working toward a solution to the problem would be concerned with the efficient use of public dollars. At the same time, efficiency certainly would not be the only issue that would shape our consideration of the potential alternatives. In addition to cost, the decision makers would probably also be concerned about the likely overall effectiveness of the potential COAs, the associated longer term prospects for the homeless individuals in question, political feasibility, fairness to the homeless individuals, and the potential difficulties associated with the implementation of each COA. While efficiency is generally a major concern in policy analysis, these other concerns can be just as important to the decision maker or more so, depending upon the context in which the decision is being made.

With all of this in mind, we find that there is no limit to the potential evaluative criteria that we might need to consider in making our policy decisions. As such, MAA allows us to incorporate quantitative, qualitative, and normative criteria into one analytic framework for assessment and comparison. In our precise definition of our problem and in the generation of our short list of potential COAs, we have already identified a tentative list of criteria that we want to consider in our assessment of the alternatives. As is the case with CBA, however, we reserve the right to adjust our list of evaluative criteria during our identification of advantages and disadvantages in the application of MAA.

5.2 Identifying the Advantages and Disadvantages

Armed once again with our short list of clearly defined potential COAs and our tentative list of evaluative criteria, we aim next to identify all of the different advantages and disadvantages that correspond to the various potential COAs on our short list. As is with CBA, while we already have evaluative criteria in mind at this point in the analytic process, we once again approach the generation of these lists of potential COA advantages and disadvantages unconstrained by those criteria. This means that we list every potential advantage and disadvantage of the COAs we can imagine, regardless of whether we expect the particular consequences of the attributes to be positive, negative, quantifiable, qualifiable, intangible, or normative in character. Likewise, our goal here once again is to think through the potential implications of the various COAs in detail in order to identify all of the results of the COA that we can. We do our best to keep an open mind throughout this step of the process, whether or not it is already the case that one of the COAs seems more attractive to us than others. We are not yet evaluating the potential COAs.

This important step in MAA, like the rest of the process, is iterative, and we can use the identification of COA advantages and disadvantages to hone our list of criteria, the COAs on our short list, or our basic problem definition as needed. In this sense we are working hard to make sure that all of the pieces fit together logically with the other segments of the analysis so that they all work in mutual support of one another, in accordance with the basic scientific method on which the analysis is based. It is not uncommon for this step in the process to suggest previously unconsidered or undefined criteria that will turn out to be very important to us as we work our way through our policy problem.

At this point then, just as was the case in CBA, we pause to review our results once we have identified all of the advantages and disadvantages of the various COAs. We ask ourselves whether we are still confident in our choice of analytic technique, and we also check to see whether or not our lists of COA advantages and disadvantages are mutually exhaustive and complete. Once we are satisfied that we have identified all of the potential COA advantages and disadvantages that we can, we then turn our attention to the selection and weighting of our evaluative criteria according to identified advantages and disadvantages, a critical last step before assessing the alternatives.

5.3 Criteria Selection and Weighting

During the course of defining the problem and generating our short list of potential courses of action, we began to specify in our minds a list of characteristics that we would like to find in any solution to our problem that we would adopt. Using our lists of advantages and disadvantages corresponding to the various short list COAs, we can expand, clarify, and finalize that list of evaluative criteria. Essentially, this step in the analytical process involves examining the lists of advantages and disadvantages to identify any additional significant criteria that we will expect to see in a solution to the policy problem.

It is important to note here that an important distinction between the verbs "want" and "need" applies in our determination of these criteria. It is important that we differentiate between the solution features that we "need," a designation meaning that any potential solution lacking in that quality would be unfeasible and therefore rejected out of hand, and those qualities that we "want," or would like to see but could live without if necessary. Once we settle upon the characteristics that we need to have present in our solution, we examine our short list of potential COAs again with these features in mind to decide whether our list should be culled any further in light of those needed criteria.

While we can select any and all criteria to include in our deliberations, generally we will want to limit our evaluative criteria to the essential considerations, or criteria that relate directly to the problem as we have defined it. These essential criteria differ widely from problem to problem, but some tend to show up more often than others. For example, most policy changes cost money to implement, and not all potential COAs provide equally effective solutions to our problems. With these two ideas in mind, we usually select first for our list the evaluative criteria of cost and effectiveness, as we nearly always seek to achieve efficiency and effectiveness in any solution that we adopt. Similarly, in political decision making we are often concerned with the political feasibility of any solution, which often varies from COA to COA, and we are also often concerned with the relative difficulties associated with the implementation of the new policies, regardless of the problem area. Other common evaluative criteria include fairness, timeliness, and enforceability, among other policy attributes.

Once we have selected our final list of evaluative criteria based upon our problem definition and the lists of COA advantages and disadvantages, we turn our attention to the weighting of those criteria. In this step of the problem-solving process, we decide how important the respective evaluative criteria are relative to one another. In some cases, we will judge the criteria to be equally important across the board; whereas in others some criteria will overshadow the others by a large margin. The way that we quantify the relationships among the criteria is through simple arithmetic multiples. For example, if we judge that "cost" is twice as important as "feasibility," we simply identify the "cost" criterion as counting twice as much as the "feasibility" criterion. An example of such weighting is included in Table 5.1. These relative weightings will eventually serve as the multiples that we use to calculate our final estimates of the desirability of the various potential COAs. After finalizing our list of evaluative criteria and the relative weighting of those criteria, we are ready to begin the process of assessing the potential COAs as we work toward our final policy recommendation.

5.4 Data Collection and Assumptions

As in CBA, we use our lists of COA advantages and disadvantages as the basis for our assessment of the desirability of the various potential COAs. However, in the case of MAA, this process differs a bit in that while the analyst using CBA seeks to identify all of the advantages and disadvantages that might translate into a tangible corresponding cost or benefit, the analyst using MAA has a different goal in mind. The MAA analyst uses the lists of potential advantages and disadvantages and other relevant evidence that she gathers in order to generate a criterion value for each of the evaluative criteria as they relate to the various potential COAs. That is, whereas the CBA analyst aims at identifying all of the tangible costs and benefits to arrive at her assessment of the COAs, the MAA analyst instead assesses the COAs more directly in light of the various criteria. Therefore, while the CBA analyst ordinarily uses each potential advantage or disadvantage from those lists only once in identifying a corresponding cost or benefit, the MAA analyst has to scan the COA advantages and disadvantages a number of times to see how each advantage or disadvantage might affect each of the various criteria. So while the CBA analyst works through the lists of advantages and disadvantages one line at a time, the MAA analyst instead works through the whole list once for each criterion for each COA.

As is also the case in CBA, some additional empirical evidence will be needed to substantiate the criteria values in MAA. Once again, however, our careful definition of the problem, potential COAs, and now evaluative criteria will enable us to gather the relevant evidence quickly and efficiently. At the same time, we are again making predictions about the likely effects of proposed future actions, and therefore we will have to leaven our empirical evidence with reasonable assumptions. Given the challenges of uncertainty, any time that we can use empirical evidence as the basis for our criteria assessments, we are better off than we are if we use assumption or reasoning alone, but particularity means that we will have to make assumptions nevertheless. We identify and carefully scrutinize those assumptions as we prepare to assign criteria values for each of the potential COAs in light of the advantages and disadvantages, the evidence we have gathered, and those critical assumptions that we have made.

5.5 Assessing Criteria Values

Using our empirical evidence, judgment, and assumptions then, we next assign criteria values for each of the evaluative criteria as they relate to the respective potential COAs on our short list. This exercise will be more precise or exact for some criteria and less so for others. For example, we might be able to get a very solid estimate of the "cost" associated with a potential COA, identifying a specific cost in dollars that we expect to absorb should we select that alternative, based upon solid supporting empirical evidence. On the other hand, we may only have a more general idea of the "feasibility" associated with the actual implementation of the alternatives, meaning that we have to rely more upon our judgment and assumptions as the basis of the criterion estimates for each COA.

Once we have assigned criteria values for each of the COAs, we then convert each of those values into a common scale. This common scale can be a numeric scale such as a scale from 1 to 5 or a "plus/minus" scale or some other gradation. The key point here is that all of those various criteria values, regardless of unit of measure, must be translated into a common scale with a common orientation. This means that if we have converted our estimate of "cost" and our "feasibility" scale into the same standard scale of 1 to 5, then we have to check to make sure that for both measures the value of 5 represents the same thing, either "best" or "worst." The common scale is what enables us to compare different mixes of the various criteria in order to determine the optimal combination that we will recommend.

5.6   Tallying the Results

Having converted our criteria values into the common scale, we then calculate our measure of the overall desirability of the various potential COAs based on those criteria values and the criteria weightings. Table 5.1 shows an example of one such calculation. Again, the purpose of the summary table is to capture the analysis in a readily accessible format that summarizes the respective advantages and disadvantages of the potential COAs in one compact medium. While the summary can stand alone in one sense, it is also understood that it only represents and combines the supporting analysis and is aimed at summarizing the critical considerations and choices that will confront the decision maker. Table 5.1 shows that COA 1 appears to be the most desirable course of action, meaning that it offers the best available combination of the key evaluative criteria.

Generally speaking, we compare the potential COAs to the status quo option as a baseline. With this in mind, we may find that no options are desirable compared to the baseline status quo option, or we may find that two or more options are more desirable

Table 5.1

An Example of a Multi-Attribute Analysis Summary Table

Educational Policy Decision

	Criterion 1 (cost)	Criterion 2 (effectiveness)	Criterion 3 (political feasibility)	Criterion 4 (ease of implementation)	Criterion 5 (fairness)	Overall desirability
COA 1 (increased testing)	3 (9)	7 (21)	8 (16)	4 (4)	10 (20)	70
COA 2 (merit pay)	3 (9)	5 (15)	5 (10)	4 (4)	8 (16)	54
COA 3 (tenure changes)	10 (30)	3 (9)	3 (6)	6 (6)	2 (4)	55
COA 4 (status quo)	8 (24)	1 (3)	7 (14)	10 (10)	6 (12)	63
Criteria weighting	x 3	x 3	x 2	x 1	x 2	

Note: This table uses a scale from 1 to 10, with 10 representing "very desirable" or "excellent." COA = course of action.

than the status quo. In the former case, this finding is just as important as if we had found desirable options, since the decision to maintain the status quo policies in place is an important decision in its own right. On the other hand, in the latter case of multiple desirable options we would make our policy recommendation based on the mutual exclusivity of the desirable options, the magnitude of resources available to support the policy changes, and our estimate of the overall feasibility of this potential broader change. We keep the "law of unintended consequences" in mind as we sort through these additional issues. Nevertheless, at this point we are again one last but important step away from being prepared to decide upon our policy recommendation.

5.7 Sensitivity and Assumption Analysis

Sensitivity and assumption analysis in MAA is very similar to that of CBA. That is, again we are concerned with identifying the most critical assumptions that we have made in generating our estimates of the desirability of the alternatives, and we again apply the "best case/worst case" test to those critical judgments. We then confront the choices posed by the results of our sensitivity analysis, revisiting the various steps of the analytical process as necessary to satisfy ourselves that we have made the best choices we could have made throughout our policy analysis. Again, in the case of questionable or ambiguous key assumptions, we may choose to trade likely validity for minor advantages in desirability of outcome, depending on the nature of our results. We do the best that we can in the face of ever-present uncertainty, but the risks that we accept are calculated rather than blind ones. If we have applied the analytic process in good faith, we are now prepared to make a policy recommendation that is as objective and as rational as we can make it.

5.8 Notes and Supplementary Readings

• Chapters 3 through 5 of Michiel S. DeVries's *Calculated Choices in Policy-Making* (1999) focus upon the selection, weighting, and validity of the criteria that we use to assess our policy alternatives. The author offers a systematic, thorough, and thoughtful approach to this critical step in multi-attribute analysis.

• Peter Kennedy offers a rigorous yet accessible guide to advanced statistical estimation techniques in *A Guide to Econometrics* (1998). Econometrics allows for the estimation of parameter values for cases in which there are multiple independent variables theorized to have an impact upon our dependent variable of interest. In chapters 1 and 2, Kennedy describes the characteristics we look for in our estimating mechanisms, the ordinary least squares method of estimation, maximum likelihood estimation, the limits of the models, alternative approaches to estimation, and other aspects of these statistical methods.

• Stuart S. Nagel addresses the methods of optimizing and the techniques of sensitivity analysis in detail in chapter 7 of *Policy Studies: Integration and Evaluation* (1988), and he elaborates upon various techniques of mathematical optimization in chapter 10 of the book.

• Stuart S. Nagel, in chapter 5 of his edited volume *Improving Policy Analysis* (1980) addresses the importance of political feasibility as a criterion in the consideration of policy alternatives. He argues that policy analysis that relies on "political science" at the expense of "public administration" is destined to fail during implementation. In chapter 10 of the same book, Peter House and Joseph Coleman expand upon the differences between the "textbook" view of policy analysis and the realities of analysis as it usually happens.

• In their edited volume *Public Policy and Statistics: Case Studies from RAND* (2000), Sally C. Morton and John E. Rolph offer relatively brief examples of executive summaries, problem definitions, and short policy recommendations.

• In chapter 6 of *Ethics in Policy Analysis* (1986) Rosemarie Tong addresses the professional obligations of the analyst in his or her relationship with the decision maker or client. She summarizes Bayles's five models of the professional–client relationship, including "agency," "contract," "friendship," "paternalism," and "fiduciary" relationships. The book also explores the role of values in policy analysis.

• In *Contemporary Public Policy Analysis* (1984), Stuart S. Nagel describes the particular challenges of sensitivity analysis in multi-attribute analyses, and he lists some of the likely sources of potential errors in those types of analysis. In chapter 3 of the text, Nagel offers a hypothetical example of the differences in policy recommendations that might result from the choice of money-centered criteria versus "nonmonetary variables." In chapter 5, Nagel describes the increasingly common question of trade-offs between equity and efficiency prevalent in public policy debates of the 1980s and later.

• In chapter 5 of Frank P. Scioli Jr. and Thomas J. Cook's *Methodologies for Analyzing Public Policies* (1975), Virginia Gray analyzes the respective advantages and disadvantages of the use of time series analysis and cross-sectional studies in policy analysis.

6

Articulating the Recommendation

6.1 The Elements of an Effective Recommendation

With the results of our analysis in hand, we are ready to prepare and deliver our policy recommendation. While we have completed the "heavy lifting" at this point in the project, a few important tasks remain. We have to articulate our policy recommendation clearly, and we need to ensure that we have complied with the decision maker's guidance for the analysis, including both formal and informal direction. Effective policy analysts take the time to tailor their message to the intended audience, and they pause at the end of their work to make sure that their policy recommendations include all of the elements needed to make a compelling case for their position on the issue in question.

Effective policy recommendations usually share a number of common characteristics. The policy recommendation begins with an *executive summary*—or overview of the issue, analysis, and recommendation—which summarizes the analysis that will follow. This executive summary serves two purposes. First, it helps the reader to understand both the argument that the analyst is about to make as well as the analytical framework that was used to solve the problem at hand. Second, the executive summary serves the practical purpose of giving the busy decision maker the opportunity to digest the analysis in a short amount of time if an immediate decision is required on the policy problem. Over time, as we demonstrate our propensity to produce rational, objective, and effective analyses routinely, this executive summary may become the only analytical product that the decision maker ever reads, trusting that the balance of the analysis is correct. Regardless of the scope of the problem, we usually try to limit the executive summary to two pages of prose. Therefore, we highlight our recommendation, the method of analysis, the key criteria, and our compelling evidence in our executive summary.

After the executive summary, our policy recommendation generally follows the basic analytical framework in its organization, as we outline the results of each step of the process concisely, precisely, and completely. We begin with our precise *definition of the problem*, as we define the relevant key terms while providing compelling empirical evidence to substantiate the claim that a problem exists. We also aim to identify the essence of the problem, as the underlying causes of our condition will dictate the effectiveness of potential solutions to the problem. Based upon our careful definition of the problem, we next describe the *potential courses of action* (COAs) available to us, summarizing the process through which we arrived at our short list of potential COAs. We also make sure to describe the reasons why we eliminated certain COAs from consideration at this point in the analysis.

In the next section of our policy recommendation, we outline the *major advantages and disadvantages* that correspond to each of the potential COAs that made it onto our short list. This is not to say that we rehash every advantage or disadvantage that we identified in this step of the analytical process. Instead, our goal here is to provide insight into the respective upsides and downsides of the various COAs in order to set the stage for the translation of those upsides and downsides into COA assessments that correspond to our evaluative criteria. In other words, our goal here is to continue the logical, sequential, and persuasive argument that we are building in support of our policy recommendation. The recommendation itself is our thesis, and all of these sections of the policy recommendation are aimed toward the objective of convincing the reader that the recommendation is compelling, logical, and correct.

Similarly, we not only summarize our *evaluative criteria* in the next portion of our policy recommendation, but we also justify the selection of those criteria based upon the problem definition, our generation of COAs, and the major advantages and disadvantages that we have identified. In the case of multi-attribute analysis (MAA), we also take the time in our prose to substantiate the *weighting of the various criteria*. We spend time here because this aspect of our analysis has a great influence on the results that we generate, and we understand that the decision maker is likely to have strong feelings about what is "most important" in arriving at a policy decision.

The next section of the policy recommendation is just as critical, as it is here that we lay out the methods we used to *predict the likely consequences of each course of action* in terms of those evaluative criteria. In many respects, this section is the heart of our analysis, and it is important that we are clear, focused, and comprehensive in our description of the logic we used to arrive at the predictions that we did. It is also important here that we delineate between the *empirical evidence, reasoning, and critical assumptions* that combined to result in our criteria values. We summarize the respective potential COAs in *a table* that captures the gist of our analysis to enable the decision maker to visualize the options available and the relative merits of those options. The next section then addresses the *sensitivity of the assumptions and predictions* that you have made, with the final section of the policy recommendation reiterating *the overall policy recommendation* that you first put forth in the executive summary. Depending upon whether or not they have been addressed previously, it may also be appropriate at this point for the analyst to comment upon the *likely obstacles to implementation* of the policy recommendation.

6.2 Articulating Your Recommendation

In terms of style, policy analysts aim to achieve a direct, concise, and precise manner of writing. Policy analysts write in a rational and thoughtful style, and they are careful to document their sources and other empirical evidence completely. They lay out their arguments in an orderly way, and they ensure that their analysis is complete while following a logical sequence from point to point. Successful analysts avoid the passive voice in their writing, and they also proofread their writing carefully, understanding that grammatical errors or other similar problems undermine their credibility as policy analysts. Similarly, it is very important that policy analysts avoid editorializing in their prose, as we aim to offer a dispassionate, rational, and objective analysis of the issue at hand, rather than the biased rationalization of a policy advocate.

Additionally, the policy analyst chooses the medium best suited to articulating the policy recommendation clearly and effectively. Some techniques include a formal decision briefing, a memorandum, a formal paper, or informal discussions, among others. The policy analyst may or may not need to show all of the steps of the analysis, and this choice is based upon the decision maker's expectations, the time available, the magnitude of the decision to be made, the relationship between the analyst and decision maker, and other such contextual factors. In any event, we tailor our presentation to the audience and the circumstances, ensuring that the "level of the pitch" corresponds correctly to the language, understanding, and knowledge of the policy area common to the audience that will receive the analysis. Effective analysts take the time to think through these issues, and they are rewarded for this thoughtfulness with a receptive audience that will readily grasp and appreciate the direction that the analyst intends to take them.

6.3 Decision Maker Considerations

As part of this careful articulation of our analytical message, we also consider the attributes of the decision maker. In fact, as mentioned throughout this book, the decision maker will shape the analytic effort formally and informally from the outset, and it is always worthwhile to take the time to think through this aspect of the analytic problem as well. Decision makers come with different temperaments, varying levels of understanding of the issue area in question, and different management styles, and all of these factors will have an impact on the eventual success and utility of the analysis that you perform. Some decision makers will expect frequent consultation throughout the analytical process, while others will expect to see you only at the beginning and the end of the project. Some decision makers will structure your problem carefully from the start, offering solution parameters and imposing working assumptions as you begin the problem-solving process. Others will take a "blue sky" approach, charging the analyst to think broadly in order to encourage creativity while planning to impose constraints at the end of the process. Furthermore, some decision makers are willing to share sensitive information with the analyst at the outset of the problem-solving process in order to facilitate the analyst's understanding of the problem, while others keep similar information to themselves for personal or political reasons. In any event, it is not uncommon for the decision maker to have defined a problem one way to the analyst, only to structure it in his or her own mind in a completely different way. The bottom line here is that while the analyst has little or no control over these decision-maker characteristics, it is always worthwhile to spend some time thinking about them. We take time to think through the decision maker's incentives, motives, and perspectives on the task at hand, even as we strive to achieve a rational and objective solution regardless of those "external" considerations.

6.4 Your Ego and Your Position

So at the end of the day, when the analysis is complete and the discussion is done, the decision maker is going to make a decision in light of your analysis, his or her own judgment, and other factors of which you may or may not be aware. Sometimes these decisions will go your way, and sometimes they will not. Sometimes the decision will be predicated upon your careful and thoughtful analysis, and sometimes the choice will be made in spite of that careful analysis. The point here is that you will win some and you will lose some. Because we live and work in a political world, not all decisions will be made on the basis of rational analysis, and we go into the problem-solving process understanding that this is the case.

Therefore, for these and other reasons it is important that we separate our egos from our policy positions. That is, avoid putting yourself in the position where you find that you have so closely married yourself to a policy position that you will find it difficult if not impossible to support the decision maker's choice without embarrassment or a loss of credibility. Decision makers will decide to go in a direction different than the one that you have proposed on occasion, and the dispassionate but rational analyst is one who expresses his misgivings but then supports the decision that is made regardless of the outcome. In the rare instances where you find yourself absolutely unable to support a decision for ethical or other reasons, you then have other choices to make, such as whether or not to resign your position or to consult with a higher authority regarding the decision. These extreme situations happen rarely, however, and therefore it is best to keep in mind that on occasion you will have to support decisions you do not like.

With all of this in mind, do not back yourself into a corner, even as you clearly and directly express your perspective on the issue in question. Avoid personalizing your policy analysis and the discussion of that analysis whenever possible. Lastly, keep in mind that policy analysis, like much of our professional lives, resembles a marathon more than it resembles a sprint. It is our track record over the long haul that eventually comes to define our reputations, and the rational and objective analyst who is careful in the application of these methods of analysis will be proven right more often than not. Introducing issues of personality into policy deliberation should happen as a conscious decision rather than a knee-jerk reaction, if it happens at all.

6.5 Notes and Supplementary Readings

• In chapter 4 of *Contemporary Public Policy Analysis* (1984), Stuart S. Nagel describes the potential problems associated with analysts' predictions of future events as well as approaches to use in describing this uncertainty and the "unknown variables" to the decision maker.

• In chapter 7 of *The Policy Process in the Modern State* (1997), Michael Hill describes the ways in which the processes of policy analysis and decision making reflect the characteristics of the organizations in which they take place. In chapter 9, Hill analyzes the particular incentives and motives of the "professional bureaucrat." In that chapter, Hill concludes by offering his perspectives on three models of "bureaucratic rationality."

• Martin Greenberger, Matthew A. Crenson, and Brian L. Crissey provide a wide variety of examples of public policy analysis in *Models in the Policy Process* (1976). Issue areas examined include national economic performance, labor/management relations, health care policies, and public safety activities. The book also provides insight into the early development of econometrics and the basic principles of policy modeling.

• In chapters 3, 4, and 5 of Arnold J. Love's edited volume, *Developing Effective Internal Evaluation* (1983), the various authors provide insights into the relationship between evaluators (analysts) and managers. In chapter 3, William D. Neigher and William Metlay outline the different competencies required for the roles of evaluator and manager, and they describe the potential problems that may arise in the relationships between the two, offering strategies for success in this area. Frederick Newman, Richard White, Deborah Zuskar, and Eric Plaut offer strategies for improving the reliability of internal evaluation data in chapter 5. In chapter 6, Gerald Landsberg describes how program utilization and service utilization studies serve as the foundation for internal evaluation in human services organizations.

• Lawrence G. Brewster and Michael E. Brown have compiled a wide variety of analyses on various contemporary public policy issues in *Public Agenda: Issues in American Politics* (1998). The policy areas covered include American political economy, education policies, health care policies, crime policies, and immigration policies.

• In chapter 8 of *The World of the Policy Analyst* (2002), Robert A. Heineman, William T. Bluhm, Steven A. Peterson, and Edward N. Kearny describe the aspects of policy analysis particular to the judicial branch of the government.

• Aaron Wildavsky and Naomi Caiden offer a book-length description of the budgeting and appropriations processes as they shape public policy deliberations in *The New Politics of the Budgetary Process* (2001). The authors demonstrate how the national budgetary climate has a major effect on the ability of policy makers to propose and champion regulatory and programmatic changes.

• David H. Rosenbloom places policy analysis and decision making into the context of public administration and agency management in *Public Administration: Understanding Management, Politics, and Law in the Public Sector* (1998). In his section on "Core Functions," Rosenbloom addresses organizational structure and process, budgeting practices, and policy analysis and decision making. George J. Gordon offers a similar treatment of this topic in chapter 13 of his book, *Public Administration in America* (1992).

• Chapter 2 of James E. Anderson's *Public Policymaking* (1997) deals with decision makers' considerations, including the policy environment, political and organizational cultures, legislators and their staffs, and others.

• Section III of Jack H. Knott and Gary J. Miller's *Reforming Bureaucracy: The Politics of Institutional Choice* (1987) analyzes differences in the nature of rationality and actor incentives within bureaucratic agencies. The book's broader focus is on describing how "reform" became the central tenet of administrative efforts in the United States since the Progressive movement in the early 1900s. The book outlines a set of institutional rules shared by bureaucratic agencies throughout American government.

7

Implementation and Beyond

7.1 Implementation

Once the policy recommendation has been considered and the decision has been made, the policy analyst may or may not be finished with his role in the problem-solving process. Some analysts help implement the chosen solution to the policy problem, and others do not. In any event, the policy analyst has a direct interest in considering how the new policy will be implemented and in observing the outcome of the implementation of that solution. The analyst's interest stems from two considerations, including the inherent challenges in bringing about organizational change, as well as the opportunity that this policy implementation offers for assessing potential future policy moves.

In the first case, the analyst aims to incorporate features into the recommended policy solution that will facilitate the successful adoption of the new policy. In the second case, the analyst understands that the implementation, supervision, and reassessment of the adopted policy choices will provide new empirical evidence for the consideration of problems likely to occur in the future in that particular policy arena. There is a rich and diverse literature that addresses these challenges and strategies of policy implementation, and some of the more prominent accounts in this literature are described in the notes for this chapter. Effective policy analysts understand that they must carefully consider the means of implementing their recommended solutions as part of the analytic process, as there is almost always a disconnect between the intentions of the policy makers and the actual policy that is implemented when all is said and done. The analyst's goal is to minimize these inevitable differences between the policy makers' intentions and the practitioners' product.

7.2   Supervision

As part of the implementation of any policy change, someone has to supervise that effort. In essence, this supervision involves articulating the vision of the change to be made, providing a blueprint or guidance to those who will make the change, ensuring that adequate resources are allocated to the effort, and seeing that the change happens according to the specified plan. While analysts will participate in this supervisory process to varying degrees in different settings, part of the process of analyzing and recommending policy changes is to facilitate the task for the personnel that will carry out that supervision. There is an art to supervision and leadership, and while there are many books devoted to those important subjects, there are a few elements of this aspect of the implementation of policy changes that merit mention here as they relate to the task of policy analysis.

To paraphrase James Q. Wilson in his effective treatment of these themes in his book *Bureaucracy* (1989), there are three critical steps in bringing about meaningful organizational change. First, the leader or supervisor must clearly articulate an explicit vision of the change or changes to be made. The leader must then ensure that the managers or organizational leaders who will actually implement the change understand this vision. Likewise, the plan to implement the policy change must include within it the means through which the performance incentives of the actual agents of the policy change are brought in line with the goals of the change itself. This last consideration might include changes in the way that performance evaluations are conducted or changes in the types of behaviors that are rewarded by the organization. If you are personally involved in supervising the implementation of the policy changes you have recommended, it is also important to think through where you will position yourself to be most effective in overseeing the process of implementation. And once that effort is under way, expect that things will not go smoothly from the start. Have a plan for reacting to bad news, and keep in mind the old saying that "first reports are usually wrong." Change usually comes with a fair share of unanticipated challenges.

7.3 Reassessment

The truth is, most of the easy solutions to our recurring challenges have already been discovered, so we generally find ourselves in the business of having to redefine our policy problems while adapting, refining, and reconfiguring our past solutions to new circumstances. Furthermore, when we add to the mix the increasing sophistication of our technologies and the corresponding added complexity of the problems and solutions that we explore in our modern context, we often find that each problem we solve is merely one segment of a larger system or process. Therefore, we are always learning and assessing, and effective analysts take advantage of the opportunities to learn afforded by the implementation of their own recommendations.

With this learning process in mind, we facilitate our assessment and reassessment of the effects of our policy changes by building mechanisms into the implementation of the policy change that provide us with periodic updates on those corresponding effects. In the health care industry, these mechanisms might include periodic patient surveys, employee climate surveys, or statistical reports regarding patient care indicators. In a corporate setting, these indicators might include customer satisfaction surveys, follow-up interviews with clients, or other means of routinely measuring organizational productivity and performance. Regardless of the type of policy area involved, however, the most effective method of assessment is to embed these various indicators in the basic operating procedures of your organization, so that they are always there to measure the status of your organization's operating climate. In sum, the effective policy analyst keeps in mind the fact that we can always get better at what we do, and that same effective analyst understands that these techniques of policy analysis are the tools that help us to achieve that progress.

7.4 Notes and Supplementary Readings

• Marilynn B. Brewer and Barry E. Collins, in their edited volume *Scientific Inquiry and the Social Sciences* (1981), elaborate upon the theme of particularity and the role of oversight and implementation in the analytic process. In chapter 10 of the book, entitled "Dilemmas in the Evaluation of Social Programs," the authors assert that local variations on the implementation of broader social programs are so idiosyncratic as to make program assessment particularly difficult. They go on to critique "outcome-oriented evaluative methods" and also offer several propositions regarding the resistance of existing programs to change and elimination.

• Aaron B. Wildavsky and Jeffrey L. Pressman elaborate on the specific challenges inherent in the translation of public policy intent into practical policy reality in *Implementation* (1984). Of particular note are their descriptions of the disparity between federal policy intentions in Lyndon Johnson's "War on Poverty" and the actual resultant administration of those policies at the local levels of government. David A. Mazmanian and Paul A. Sabatier offer another effective treatment of this same topic as it relates to the task of policy analysis in *Implementation and Public Policy* (1989).

• In chapter 6 of Frank Fischer and John Forester's edited volume, *Confronting Values in Policy Analysis* (1987), Forester offers techniques that the analyst can use in crafting courses of action that will enable the analyst to anticipate and remedy potential problems in implementing that course of action.

• In chapter 1 of *Contemporary Public Policy Analysis* (1984), Stuart S. Nagel places the task of policy analysis into the context

of effective public administration. He also describes the development of the field of policy studies to that point in the discipline's
history. In chapter 2, he goes on to describe various trends occurring in the field in terms of the goals of policy analysis, the basis
for policy makers' decisions, and the role of public institutions in
the policy-making process.

• In chapter 6 of *The Policy Process in the Modern State* (1997),
Michael Hill offers an overview of the implementation literature
and a critique of the "top-down" and "bottom-up" models of policy
implementation.

• Chapter 6 of Duncan MacRae Jr. and James A. Wilde's *Policy
Analysis for Public Decisions* (1985) addresses the impact of political feasibility on the analyst's efforts, as well as the ways that considerations of policy implementation often constrain those efforts.

• In the first four chapters of Edward R. Tufte's edited volume,
The Quantitative Analysis of Social Problems (1970), the various
authors offer critiques of different quantitative analyses that were
produced in the years prior. William G. Cochran, Frederick
Mosteller, and John W. Tukey assess the methodological choices
made by the authors of *The Kinsey Report*, while Aaron Wildavsky
analyzes the lessons learned from the Kennedy–Nixon election of
1960. In the next chapter, a host of authors join to evaluate the
methodology employed in the study of the linkage between smok-
ing and lung cancer, and Irwin D.J. Bross uses that same issue in
calling for a unifying set of statistical "rules of the game."

• In chapter 7 of Arnold J. Love's edited volume, *Developing Effective Internal Evaluation* (1983), Angela Browne and Aaron
Wildavsky discuss the consequences of carrying the dual responsibilities of implementing and evaluating programs in an organization.

• In chapter 7 of *The World of the Policy Analyst* (2002), Robert A. Heineman, William T. Bluhm, Steven A. Peterson, and

Edward N. Kearny comment on the implications of the 1994 elections for public policy making. The authors also analyze the increasing state-level influence within national policy making and the impact of think tanks and private-sector policy groups that they see within the policy-making process today.

• In chapter 8 of David H. Rosenbloom's *Public Administration: Understanding Management, Politics, and Law in the Public Sector* (1998), the author describes the relationship between policy analysis and the evaluation of organizational implementation of the policy decisions made.

• Richard J. Stillman Jr. offers a wide variety of selections describing public administration choices made in *Public Administration: Concepts and Cases* (1996). These cases and issue areas include mine safety, intergovernmental relations, internal organizational dynamics, public budgeting, prison policies, foreign policy, and other sample cases.

• Joel D. Aberbach analyzes and describes the increasingly difficult task facing congressional overseers in *Keeping a Watchful Eye* (1990).

• Charles E. Lindblom lists reasons why bureaucratic agencies so often fail to implement specified policies properly in chapter 8 of *The Policymaking Process* (1980). Among the reasons he cites are incomplete policy specifications, conflicting criteria for policy application, conflicting leader directives, limited actor competence, and inadequate resources for policy administration, among others. Lindblom goes on to differentiate between public-sector and private-sector organizational politics.

• In chapters 15 and 16 of *Policy Choices and Public Action* (1996), Charles F. Bonser, Eugene B. McGregor Jr., and Clinton V. Oster Jr. analyze the nature of trends in governmental reforms over the last century. The authors offer an assessment of the challenges facing government administrators in their efforts to bring about meaningful change in the federal government's policy-making machinery.

• Chapters 6, 7, and 8 of Patrick Dunleavy's *Democracy, Bureaucracy, and Public Choice* (1991) examine various models of bureaucratic actor behaviors and the incentives that usually exist in bureaucratic settings. Dunleavy's focus is on providing an economic explanation to the policy-making process. Douglass C. North approaches the subject of institutional evolution and organizational learning from the same perspective in his book, *Institutions, Institutional Change, and Economic Performance* (1990).

• In *Reinventing Government: How the Entrepreneurial Spirit is Transforming the Public Sector* (1992), David Osborne and Ted Gaebler provide insights into a variety of techniques that can be used to facilitate successful implementation of policy changes as they are made. Most of their prescriptions involve changing the basic incentives of government actors at appropriate levels, an effort tailored to the mission, staffs, and culture of the agency in question.

• In James Q. Wilson's *Bureaucracy: What Government Agencies Do and Why They Do It* (1989), the author provides insights into the effect of organizational culture on policy outcomes and implementation. Wilson then suggests strategies by which organizational leaders can go about reshaping that organizational culture and the incentives, procedures, and rules within it to bring it in line with the larger goals of the organization. This book is helpful for any analyst aiming to incorporate mechanisms for tracking the success of proposed policy changes within the body of the policy recommendation itself. Wilson also provides examples of the techniques that he suggests in a variety of policy areas, including defense policy, prison policies, education, and others.

Bibliography

Aberbach, Joel D. *Keeping a Watchful Eye: The Politics of Congressional Oversight*. Washington, DC: Brookings, 1990.

Anderson, James E. *Public Policymaking*, 3d ed. Boston: Houghton Mifflin, 1997.

Bardach, Eugene. *A Practical Guide to Policy Analysis*. New York: Chatham House, 2000.

Benn, S.I., and G.W. Mortimore, editors. *Rationality and the Social Sciences*. London: Routledge and Kegan Paul, 1978.

Bonser, Charles F., Eugene B. McGregor Jr., and Clinton V. Oster Jr. *Policy Choices and Public Action*. Upper Saddle River, NJ: Prentice Hall, 1996.

———. *American Public Policy Problems: An Introductory Guide*, 2d ed. Upper Saddle River, NJ: Prentice Hall, 2000.

Brewer, Garry D. and Peter deLeon. *The Foundations of Policy Analysis*. Homewood, IL: Dorsey, 1983.

Brewer, Marilynn B., and Barry E. Collins, editors. *Scientific Inquiry and the Social Sciences*. San Francisco: Jossey-Bass, 1981.

Brewster, Lawrence G., and Michael E. Brown. *The Public Agenda: Issues in American Politics*, 4th ed. New York: St. Martin's, 1998.

Brock, Bernard L., James Chesebro, John Gragus, and James Klumpp. *Public Policy Decision Making: Systems Analysis and Comparative Advantages Debate*. New York: Harper and Row, 1973.

Clemons, Randall S., and Mark K. McBeth. *Public Policy Praxis: Theory and Pragmatism: A Case Approach*. Upper Saddle River, NJ: Prentice Hall, 2001.

Cochran, Clarke E., et al. *American Public Policy*, 6th ed. New York: St. Martin's/ Worth, 1999.

Corbett, Michael. *Research Methods in Political Science: An Introduction Using MicroCase*, 4th ed. Belmont, CA: Wadsworth, 2001.

Dery, David. *Problem Definition in Policy Analysis*. Lawrence: University Press of Kansas, 1984.

DeVries, Michiel S. *Calculated Choices in Policy-Making*. New York: St. Martin's, 1999.

Dunleavy, Patrick. *Democracy, Bureaucracy, and Public Choice: Economic Explanations in Political Science*. New York: Prentice Hall, 1991.

Dunn, William N., editor. *Values, Ethics, and the Practice of Policy Analysis.* Washington, DC: Lexington, 1983.

Dye, Thomas R. *Understanding Public Policy,* 10th ed. Englewood Cliffs, NJ: Prentice Hall, 2002.

Fenno, Richard F., Jr. *Home Style: House Members in Their Districts.* New York: HarperCollins, 1978.

Fiorina, Morris P. "When Stakes Are High, Rationality Kicks In," *New York Times,* February 26, 2000, A13, A17.

Fischer, Frank, and John Forester, editors. *Confronting Values in Policy Analysis: The Politics of Criteria.* Newbury Park, CA: Russell Sage Foundation, 1987.

Fischer, Frank. *Evaluating Public Policy.* New York: Wadsworth, 1995.

Formaini, Robert. *The Myth of Scientific Public Policy.* London: Transaction, 1990.

Frankfort-Nachmias, Chava, and David Nachmias. *Research Methods in the Social Sciences,* 6th ed. New York: Worth, 2000.

Fry, Brian R. *Mastering Public Administration.* Chatham, NJ: Chatham House, 1989.

Gordon, George J. *Public Administration in America,* 4th ed. New York: St. Martin's, 1992.

Greenberger, Martin, Matthew A. Crenson, and Brian L. Crissey. *Models in the Policy Process: Public Decision Making in the Computer Era.* New York: Russell Sage Foundation, 1976.

Guess, George M., and Paul G. Farnham. *Cases in Public Policy Analysis,* 2d ed. Washington, DC: Georgetown University Press, 2000.

Hakim, Catherine. *Research Design: Successful Designs for Social and Economic Research,* 2d ed. New York: Routledge, 2000.

Hawkesworth, M.E. *Theoretical Issues in Policy Analysis.* Albany, NY: SUNY Press, 1988.

Heineman, Robert A., William T. Bluhm, Steven A. Peterson, and Edward N. Kearny. *The World of the Policy Analyst: Rationality, Values, and Politics,* 3d ed. New York: Chatham House, 2002.

Hill, Michael. *The Policy Process in the Modern State,* 3d ed. New York: Prentice Hall, 1997.

Irwin, Lewis G. *A Chill in the House: Actor Perspectives on Change and Continuity in the Pursuit of Legislative Success.* Albany, NY: SUNY Press, 2002.

Johnston, J. *Econometric Methods,* 3d ed. New York: McGraw-Hill, 1984.

Jreisat, Jamil E. *Comparative Public Administration and Policy.* Boulder, CO: Westview, 2002.

Kennedy, Peter. *A Guide to Econometrics,* 4th ed. Boston: MIT Press, 1998.

King, Anthony, editor. *The New American Political System.* Washington, DC: American Enterprise Institute, 1978.

King, Gary, Robert O. Keohane, and Sidney Verba. *Designing Social Inquiry: Scientific Inference in Qualitative Research.* Princeton, NJ: Princeton, 1994.

Kingdon, John W. *Agendas, Alternatives, and Public Policies,* 2d ed. New York: HarperCollins, 1994.

Knott, Jack H., and Gary J. Miller. *Reforming Bureaucracy: The Politics of Institutional Choice.* Englewood Cliffs, NJ: Prentice Hall, 1987.

Lester, James P., and Joseph Stewart Jr. *Public Policy: An Evolutionary Approach.* Minneapolis, MN: West, 1996.

Lindblom, Charles E. *The Policymaking Process*, 2d ed. Englewood Cliffs, NJ: Prentice Hall, 1980.

————. "The 'Science' of Muddling Through." *Public Administration Review*, 19 (1959): 79–88.

Love, Arnold J., editor. *Developing Effective Internal Evaluation.* San Francisco: Jossey-Bass, 1983.

MacRae, Duncan, Jr., and James A. Wilde. *Policy Analysis for Public Decisions.* Lanham, MD: University Press of America, 1985.

MacRae, Duncan, Jr. *Policy Indicators: Links Between Social Science and Public Debate.* Chapel Hill: University of North Carolina Press, 1985.

Mayhew, David R. *Congress: The Electoral Connection.* New Haven, CT: Yale, 1974.

Mazmanian, David A., and Paul A. Sabatier. *Implementation and Public Policy.* Lanham, MD: University Press of America, 1989.

Mitton, Lavinia, Holly Sutherland, and Melvyn Weeks, editors. *Microsimulation Modelling for Policy Analysis: Challenges and Innovations.* Cambridge, UK: Cambridge University Press, 2000.

Morton, Sally C., and John E. Rolph, editors. *Public Policy and Statistics: Case Studies From RAND.* Ann Arbor, MI: Springer, 2000.

Munger, Michael C. *Analyzing Policy: Choices, Conflicts, and Practices.* New York: Norton, 2000.

Nachmias, David, editor. *The Practice of Policy Evaluation.* New York: St. Martin's, 1980.

Nagel, Stuart S. *Contemporary Public Policy Analysis.* Tuscaloosa: University of Alabama Press, 1984.

————, editor. *Improving Policy Analysis.* London: Sage, 1980.

————. *Policy Studies: Integration and Evaluation.* New York: Greenwood, 1988.

North, Douglass C. *Institutions, Institutional Change, and Economic Performance.* Cambridge, UK: Cambridge University Press, 1990.

Osborne, David, and Ted Gaebler. *Reinventing Government: How the Entrepreneurial Spirit is Transforming the Public Sector.* New York: Penguin, 1992.

Peters, B. Guy. *American Public Policy: Promise and Performance*, 5th ed. Pittsburgh: University of Pittsburgh, 2000.

Research for Public Policy: Brookings Dedication Lectures. Washington, DC: Brookings, 1961.

Rosenbloom, David H. *Public Administration: Understanding Management, Politics, and Law in the Public Sector*, 4th ed. New York: McGraw-Hill, 1998.

Scharpf, Fritz W. *Games Real Actors Play: Actor-Centered Institutionalism in Policy Research.* Boulder, CO: Westview, 1997.

Schelling, Thomas C. *Micromotives and Macrobehavior.* New York: Norton, 1978.

Schroedel, Jean Reith. *Congress, the President, and Policymaking: A Historical Analysis.* London: M.E. Sharpe, 1994.

Schwandt, Thomas A. *Qualitative Inquiry: A Dictionary of Terms.* London: Sage, 1997.

Scioli, Frank P., Jr., and Thomas J. Cook. *Methodologies for Analyzing Public Policies*. Lexington, MA: Lexington Books, 1975.

Shapiro, Ian. "A Model That Pretends to Explain Everything," *New York Times*, February 26, 2000, A13, A17.

Shepsle, Kenneth A., and Mark S. Bonchek. *Analyzing Politics: Rationality, Behavior, and Institutions*. New York: Norton, 1997.

Stillman, Richard J., Jr. *Public Administration: Concepts and Cases*, 6th ed. Geneva, IL: Houghton Mifflin, 1996.

Streeter, Paul, editor. *Values in Social Theory: A Selection of Essays on Methodology by Gunnar Myrdal*. New York: Harper and Brothers, 1958.

Stone, Deborah. *Policy Paradox: The Art of Political Decision Making*. New York: Norton, 1997.

Suchman, Edward A. *Evaluative Research: Principles and Practice in Public Service and Social Action Programs*. New York: Russell Sage Foundation, 1967.

Theodoulou, Stella A., and Matthew A. Cain, editors. *Public Policy: The Essential Readings*. Englewood Cliffs, NJ: Prentice Hall, 1995.

Tong, Rosemarie. *Ethics in Policy Analysis*. Englewood Cliffs, NJ: Prentice Hall, 1986.

Tufte, Edward R., editor. *The Quantitative Analysis of Social Problems*. Reading, MA: Addison-Wesley, 1970.

Van Evera, Stephen. *Guide to Methods for Students of Political Science*. Ithaca, NY: Cornell University, 1997.

Weaver, Frederick S. *Economic Literacy*. Lanham, MD: Rowman and Littlefield, 2002.

Weber, Linda R. *The Analysis of Social Problems*. Boston: Allyn and Bacon, 1995.

Weimer, David L., and Aidan R. Vining. *Policy Analysis: Concepts and Practice*, 3d ed. Upper Saddle River, NJ: Prentice Hall, 1999.

Wells, Donald T., and Chris R. Hamilton. *The Policy Puzzle: Finding Solutions in the Diverse American System*. Upper Saddle River, NJ: Prentice Hall, 1996.

Wildavsky, Aaron, and Jeffrey L. Pressman. *Implementation*, 3d ed. Berkeley: University of California, 1984.

Wildavsky, Aaron, and Naomi Caiden. *The New Politics of the Budgetary Process*, 4th ed. New York: Addison Wesley Longman, 2001.

Wilson, James Q. *Bureaucracy: What Government Agencies Do and Why They Do It*. New York: Basic Books, 1989.

Index

About the Author

Lewis G. Irwin is an assistant professor of public policy and political science at Duquesne University. He is the author of *A Chill in the House* (2002), a book about changes in the U.S. House of Representatives over the last several decades, as well as other works on various aspects of legislative politics and public policy. Irwin received his doctorate from Yale University, and he is also a graduate of the U.S. Military Academy and a veteran of Operation "Desert Storm."